C000152661

A guide to

FUN WAYS TO FUNDRAISE

for your community, church or charity

Penny Hallett

© 2015 Penny Hallett. All rights reserved.

No part of this publication may be reproduced, stored in a retrieval system or transmitted in any form or by any means, electronic, mechanical, photocopying, recording or otherwise, without the prior written permission of the author.

The information in this book is intended for general information, and does not constitute professional or legal advice.

Every reasonable effort has been made to ensure that the information in this book is as accurate and up to date as possible at the time of publishing. However, specific details of the relevant UK legislation have been omitted in an attempt to simplify the issues. Any information contained in this book does not therefore constitute a definitive or complete statement of the law. You should always seek independent legal and professional advice in relation to specific fundraising events, activities or other proposals.

To the fullest extent permitted by law, the author excludes all liability for loss or damage arising out of or in connection with your use of this book. No responsibility or liability for any errors or omissions or for any loss or damage occasioned to any person acting, or refraining from any action, as a result of any material within this publication, will be accepted by the author.

This book includes contact details for organisations. Such details may have changed or become defunct since the date of publication. It is your responsibility to check that the contact details are correct and the author accepts no responsibility or liability for any losses or damages you may incur if you fail to do so.

This book also includes references to external websites. The author has no control or responsibility for such websites, their content or availability. The author makes no representations as regards the availability, accuracy, content or suitability of such websites, or any material found on them, or any results that may be obtained from using them. The author does not accept any responsibility or liability for the advice, information, products or services contained on any external websites referred to in this book. If you decide to access any of these websites, you do so entirely at your own risk.

ISBN: 1502924226
ISBN 13: 9781502924223

Contents

Chapter 3
Music, movies and dancing 40

CONTENTS

Acknowledgements

My heartfelt thanks go to everyone who has given their time, expertise and support to this book, in particular: Debbie Bambridge, Marcus and Tanya Booth, Ashley Borthwick, the Rev. Martin Gordon, David Marder, Dominic Moody, Karen Needham, Debbie Pugh-Jones, Nicky Strong, Jane Watkivs, Rob Wicks and staff at Child-Safe, the Gambling Commission and the Institute of Fundraising.

Special thanks to South Gloucestershire Council's Trading Standards & Licensing team for their help in preparing this guide, particularly to Chris Jones, whose expert advice and information helped clarify many complex licensing issues and to Ewen Macgregor, Licensing Partner at Bond Dickinson, for his expert guidance on the law.

Illustrations by Dave McCann
(www.cargocollective.com/davedrawings)

All royalties from the sale of this book are being donated to the St Michael's Church Heart of the Community project. The £5.5m project will provide a new, multi-purpose church and community centre, restore the medieval church and refurbish the Old School Rooms at Stoke Gifford, South Gloucestershire, UK.

St Michael's Church Centre Ltd is a registered charity no: 1149601.

Introduction

Giving up a bit of your time to raise money for charity and support your community can make a big difference to the lives of others.

With a little bit of imagination, all sorts of things can be turned into simple fundraising activities and events.

This book has been written for non-professional fundraisers seeking to support churches, community groups, schools, hospices, amateur sports clubs and drama groups, as well as individuals looking to raise money for local or national charities.

Inside you'll find lots of fundraising ideas, from a baked beans bath to a pub sports day, tips on how to get going and pitfalls to beware of. Some activities may raise less than a tenner, others thousands of pounds, but successful fundraising will yield more than money.

Whatever you decide to do – however big or small – your activity or event will raise awareness of your charity or project, help create the funds to make it happen and provide an ideal opportunity to meet and get to know people.

The more innovative your idea or event the better – not only will it help you stand out from the crowd, it will increase its appeal to the people you want to attract and give a real buzz to your publicity. Try to think outside the box. Get together with friends, relatives and fellow fundraisers and bounce ideas off each other. If you can't come up with a completely new idea, think about how you could adapt a tried and tested fundraiser by turning it on its head or by simply changing the venue, timing or other feature. A bike carry instead of a bike ride, a murder mystery night in the cellars (dungeons!) of an old house or a Christmas fair in the middle of summer?

Fundraising can be hard work, but above all, fundraising should be FUN. The most successful events work well because everyone is having a great time and if people are enjoying themselves they'll be far more willing to donate money or learn more about what you're trying to achieve.

Good luck!

1
Twelve steps to successful fundraising

Eager to get going? Tempting as it is to jump straight in and start organising, time spent planning will pay dividends.

1. What are my objectives?

What are you looking to achieve? Is your main aim to raise money, create awareness of your charity, project or organisation, motivate existing supporters, attract new donors or build community?

A single, clear objective will help you determine who to invite, your fundraising target, your ticket price and your venue. If your objective is to combat loneliness among the elderly by inviting them to get together for a lunch or quiz, then you may only want to recover your costs. If your main objective, however, is to raise as much as possible for your charity or cause, you'll need to ensure you make enough to cover your costs and sufficient profit to make the effort worthwhile.

You may well have more than one objective – but be clear which is your primary objective. For instance, you may want to hold a harvest celebration to encourage the community to get involved in your church's activities as well as raise funds for a specific project. If your main objective is to engage with the community, then your ticket price will need to be set to make your event accessible to as many people as possible. If your primary objective is to make money, you'll want to consider a higher ticket price.

The type of activity or event you run – and how it is run – will affect the character and reputation of your charity or cause. Check that your objectives and activities are compatible with the values and vision of the organisation you're supporting. Tarot card readings, for instance, are unlikely to be appropriate for church fundraising activities and events involving gambling or alcohol may not find favour with organ-isations supporting people with addictions.

2. What's my big idea?

Pick a fundraising idea that appeals to you. It doesn't have to be overly ambitious, just something that you feel you can achieve and that you, your helpers and your guests will enjoy.

Proud gardeners may want to open their gardens to the public, keen cooks might like to bake up a few treats to sell, and the more extrovert might be willing – or even like – to go to work with half a moustache or a half-shaved head in return for sponsorship.

How popular will the event be with the people in your area, workplace or school? What skills and interests can you draw on from your friends and supporters? Talk to the people whose help you'd need to make it happen and ask them what they think.

Once you've chosen your activity or event, think about how you can build on it. Many events, however small, will become more attractive by adding food. Serving hot drinks, cakes and biscuits, a supper, lunch or dinner, will encourage more people to attend and will boost your profits.

As soon as people arrive at your event, or take an interest in what you're doing, you'll have a captive audience. Use this opportunity to maximise the take by combining as many ways of raising money as possible while you've got your audience present. Why not complement your cake sale with a raffle or 'guess the weight of the cake' competition, hold a silent auction at your murder mystery night, add a quiz to your barbecue or a book sale to your coffee morning?

Think of ways to make your event stand out by making it that little bit different. Pick a theme – even if it's just a colour scheme – which you can carry through to your decorations, tickets, publicity and even the refreshments.

A simple afternoon tea, for example, could become a 'spring fling' or how about a vintage or Alice in Wonderland theme – complete with your own Alice, Mad Hatter and Queen of Hearts?

3. When should I do it?

Allow yourself plenty of time to recruit your team and organise your activity.

Weekends tend to be best for community events and Fridays are good for fundraising at work or school. If it's just after pay day, so much the better.

Check websites and guides which list events in your area to find out what else is going on. You don't want to hold your summer fair on the same day as the local school.

Check there are no major sporting fixtures which could clash with your activity and take school holidays into account.

Other people's events may also provide an opportunity for you. If you're planning a cake or handicrafts sale, or like the idea of a bit of welly wanging, why not approach the organiser of another event and ask if you can piggyback on their event – for nothing or in return for a small fee.

Write down every activity you will need to undertake from hiring the venue to booking entertainers, printing publicity material and clearing up afterwards. Have you given yourself enough time? Draw up a timeline and refer to it constantly to check everything is going according to plan.

4. Where should I do it?

It's important to choose the right venue for your event. If you're organising a jumble sale, people won't be too worried about the décor, but if guests are paying a premium price for a formal dinner or show, they'll expect first class facilities. Always visit any venue before you book, even if you have used it before, to prevent any unpleasant surprises.

Picture the event, and the type of people you hope to attract, in your mind. Is the venue going to be large enough for your anticipated audience to be able to move around easily? Will everyone be able to see and hear what's going on? Is the atmosphere right for your event? Is the venue clean and well maintained? Is there suitable lighting, heating and ventilation?

Are there enough toilets and is there good access for people with a disability? How will disabled people be evacuated in an emergency without using a lift? Work out what extra facilities you may need. You don't want to turn up on the day and find you can't have access to the kitchen or there are not enough tables, chairs, glasses or crockery. Will you need somewhere safe to store cash on the day?

Try and talk to someone who has used the venue before. Ask them what worked well and if they had any problems.

Be clear about when you can gain access to the venue and the time by which you need to have vacated the premises. If you don't expect people to arrive by foot, consider parking and transport facilities.

Always read the small print – particularly any penalty if you have to cancel the booking – so you are completely clear about what you will be getting for your money.

It's always worth mentioning that your event is for charity – you may be able to negotiate a discount or even get it free.

If you want to hold your event on public land you will need to apply to the local authority – they will also be able to help with advice and information about organising outdoor events. Similarly, if you're running an outdoor event on private property, you'll need the landowner's permission.

You'll need to ensure the venue complies with legal requirements for health and safety. This is particularly relevant if you're using land or buildings which are not usually open to the public. Detailed guidance is available on the Health and Safety Executive website (www.hse.gov.uk).

Check what existing insurance cover is in place in case of injury to people or damage to property and whether it will cover your event. You may need to make your own insurance arrangements. Is the venue licensed, and if so, what activities are covered?

If you're running an outdoor event, consider what arrangements you need to make if it tips down with rain. If previous events have been held on the site, the venue organiser will be in a good position to give you an idea of the type of contingency arrangements made by previous users.

5. Who will be interested?

Think about the type of people who are likely to attend your event. Members of a local youth group, for instance, are unlikely to show much interest in attending a flower festival, but it could be a big hit with members of flower arranging and gardening clubs and societies.

The people you're hoping to attract – your target audience – will not only determine how much you charge for tickets or any additional fundraising activities but also how you publicise the event.

Your core audience is likely to be those who have already shown an interest in, or are involved with, your organisation or charity, and those who are interested in you and what you're up to. You may then want to attract their families, friends and neighbours. Once you're clear about your target audience, think about how you'll let them know about your event.

If you think students will be interested in your event, you'll want to promote the event through the Students' Union, posters, flyers, Facebook and Twitter. If you want to attract high net worth individuals to a £100-a-head fundraising dinner and dance, personal invitations would be more appropriate.

The bigger the event, the more time and money you'll need to invest to draw as many people as possible from a wide area.

6. Who can I get to help?

There are very few fundraising events where you can go it alone. Don't underestimate the amount of work involved or the number of volunteers you'll need to help with the preparations and on the day itself.

Share responsibility for organising the event with as many like-minded people as possible who you can trust and who believe in the cause or charity you're supporting. Never be afraid to ask someone to lend a hand. You'll be surprised how willing people are to help.

Try to find people with the particular skills and connections you need for your event and decide who will shoulder which responsibilities. If you're running a large event it's good practice to form a committee and allocate specific responsibilities and deadlines to each member. Be careful not to overburden people and be prepared to re-allocate work if people don't follow through on their actions or if their circumstances change and they are no longer able to help.

Get any backing and senior support you might need from your governing body, clergy, employer, head teacher or charity.

Keep in touch so everyone feels involved and confident about what they're doing and how it fits into the bigger picture.

7. Do my sums add up?

Do you want to raise a set figure or are you happy to just cover your costs? Even if making money isn't your primary objective, you will still need to make sure that your activity is run on a sound financial basis.

First, list all your expenses, for instance venue hire, catering, promotion, prizes, insurance, licences, first aid cover, signage, etc. Don't forget any hidden costs such as staffing, photocopying and distribution. Don't expect volunteers to provide free food or drink – not everyone is in the financial position to be able to donate the cost of ingredients. If they offer, that's fine.

Depending on the size of your event, add a contingency of 5–10% of your budget for any unexpected expenditure. This will give you an idea of how much you need to raise in order to break even. Next, work out how many tickets you think you will realistically be able to sell. Take advice from people you know who have run similar events. Then divide your costs by the number of tickets you expect to sell. This will give you an idea of the minimum amount you will need to charge.

Now jot down all the potential ways in which you can raise money at the event, for example through a raffle, an auction, stalls, sale of refreshments, etc. Estimate how much you think your guests will be prepared to spend at the event. Don't be tempted to overcharge or skimp on the quality of food or drink. It's important that people feel they've had a fair deal and not been ripped off.

Once you've done your sums, you may decide that the ticket price would be too high for you to be able to sell sufficient tickets to break even, or your profit would be insufficient to justify the time and trouble that you and your team would need to put in. If you decide to go ahead and find you can't sell enough tickets to break even, don't be afraid to cancel your event rather than risk making an even greater loss.

You may well need initial financial investment to get started or financial backing in case something happens and you fail to break even on the day. See if the charity or organisation you're supporting would be willing to help.

If, at the end of the event, you haven't raised as much as you'd hoped, or you feel that what you've raised doesn't reflect the amount of effort you put in, don't despair! The enjoyment of your supporters and guests will more than compensate and you may well have inspired others to run an event of their own.

8. How can I get sponsorship or other financial support?

Local firms, your suppliers, your employer or generous donors might be willing to underwrite the cost of your event, match the money you raise, or sponsor a part of your event such as the food or wine, print costs, or prizes.

Bear in mind that they are likely to be inundated with pleas for help from worthy causes. Why should they support your charity or project? Consider what's in it for them. Can you show how they, or their workforce, will benefit from involvement with your charity, project or event? Can you offer them a stall at your summer fair, a mention in your publicity, a link from your website or an acknowledgement in the event programme?

Tailor your approach to your prospective sponsor. Try and address each letter individually, ideally to the chief executive, owner or manager. If you're not sure who to write to, check on the internet or phone up and ask. If you haven't heard back within two to three weeks, contact the person you wrote to by phone or email to see if they've had time to consider your request.

If sponsors are individual donors and sign a Gift Aid declaration, registered charities and causes can claim 25p from the government for every £1 donated. Ask your charity or cause to send you a form, or download one from their website.

Generally, a small acknowledgement of support, such as a mention in a list of sponsors in a programme or on a notice, is unlikely to cause a problem. If however the sponsor wants a 'significant benefit' in return for their support, such as the event being named after them or use of their logo in promotional material, they may need to pay VAT on the donation and you would need to take this into account when negotiating any sponsorship package.

Acknowledging sponsorship is a complex area and if you are relying on sponsorship to stage your event, seek advice from your charity or HM Revenue & Customs (see Useful contacts and resources).

9. How do I make it safe and legal?

As an event organiser and a representative of your organisation or cause, you have a duty to ensure that you stay within the law. If anyone is injured because of your event or you are accused of flouting the law, it will damage not only your own reputation but that of the charity or cause you are supporting.

Don't be put off by the rules and regulations. There are regulations about serving food and alcohol, lotteries, collecting door-to-door and in the street, promoting events, showing a film and playing live and recorded music – to name just a few. There is guidance in this book and the final section lists useful sources of information and advice.

If you are in any doubt, seek professional or legal advice.

a. Insurance

Ensure that sufficient public liability insurance cover exists to indemnify yourself against civil litigation (a minimum cover of £5 million is suggested). Check with your venue first of all, as they may already have insurance that covers your event. If you don't think the insurance is sufficient, or covers all your needs, you may want to take out additional cover or obtain your own insurance. You may also want to consider taking out cancellation and/or adverse weather insurance to cover any irrecoverable costs should you have to cancel, abandon or postpone the event for any reasons beyond your control.

You will also need to ensure that you, or the charity or cause you are supporting, have insurance cover for yourself and your helpers. Any third party suppliers such as caterers and exhibitors, or people who are bringing equipment onto the site, for example bouncy castles, hog roasts and fairground rides, will need to have their own insurance cover, even if they are providing their services free of charge. Use reputable companies and ask to see a copy of their risk assessment and relevant insurance before the event and check that these provide adequate cover for your event.

Caterers and suppliers who are using moving machinery must also have the necessary health and safety certificates. Again, you should ask to see copies of these.

b. Risk assessment

You will need to consider the health and safety of people taking part in your event at the planning stage and during the event itself. A simple risk assessment for the overall event and each activity within the event, will help you to identify any potential problems and how you can take reasonable precautions to avoid them happening.

Consider everything that could go wrong on the day. List all potential risks (for instance a requirement to evacuate the venue), who is at risk (the people attending the event, particularly people with a disability), how you can mitigate against the risk (make sure exits and escape routes are kept clear and appoint fire wardens to supervise any evacuation) and who is responsible for each risk.

Take particular care if you are using any electrical equipment – make sure any lighting, amplification or other equipment is connected by a competent person or, depending on the equipment and venue, a qualified electrician. If anything looks unsafe on the day, stop the activity and do not use the equipment.

Have someone at the event who can administer first aid. The type of first aid cover you will need to provide will depend on the size and nature of your event, the risks involved and the ages and abilities of the people attending. If your event is quite large, such as a village fair or there's a greater risk of people being injured, such as an It's a Knockout tournament, you may want to consider paying a private company or a medical charity such as St John Ambulance or the Red Cross to attend. It would also be prudent to inform the local police, ambulance and fire services before the event.

For further information about event safety visit the Health and Safety Executive website (www.hse.gov.uk for Great Britain and www.hseni.gov.uk for Northern Ireland).

c. Security

Think about how to make your event secure and prevent people straying off limits. Limit the number of entry/exit points and have at least one steward at each point to keep a check on people entering and those leaving, particularly any young children who may have become separated from their parents.

If you have alcohol at your event you may also need arrangements to deal with any potential gatecrashers or people affected by alcohol.

Hopefully, your hard work will pay off and you'll be making lots of money for your charity. You may want to collect cash for safekeeping during the event, or leave it to the end. Where possible, have two people around when money is being handled and counted. Store any money in a secure container and keep a record of how much each activity raised. Take care when carrying money around the site or to the bank, and pay it into the bank as soon as possible.

d. Safeguarding children and vulnerable adults

The welfare and safety of children and young people (up to the age of 18) and adults who may be vulnerable because of their age or mental or physical health, is crucial. If you're running an event or activity for children or vulnerable adults, for instance a children's disco or a Christmas party, you should follow your organisation or charity's child protection or safeguarding policy and procedures.

It's important the level of supervision is appropriate to the number of people attending, their age group and needs. Bear in mind that you may need to increase the ratio of adults to children, depending on the experience of the supervisors and the location and nature of the event. Always try to ensure a minimum of two adults at events involving children, for the protection of both children and adults. If the participants will be of mixed gender, you should also include male and female supervisors. Always err on the side of caution.

Encourage the adult who is responsible for the child to attend the event or activity with them. If this isn't possible, try to obtain the permission of the parent or guardian, preferably in writing. Ask the parent or guardian to provide emergency contact details and, if you're serving food, information about any allergies their child might have. Your organisation or charity should be able to provide written consent forms which cover things like contact details, allergies, medication and photographs.

No staff, helpers or outside contractors, such as a children's entertainer, should be in a position where they are alone with a child outside the sight or hearing of another adult, such as taking a child to the toilet or when visiting Santa's grotto. Recruit as many volunteers or staff helpers as possible to be vigilant during the event and to ensure that children are not left alone with only one adult.

Try to use staff and helpers who have had some form of child protection awareness training. Wherever possible, use staff, helpers and contractors who have a Disclosure and Barring Service certificate (Disclosure Scotland in Scotland and AccessNi in Northern Ireland).

If you want to take photographs of children or young people at your event to send to the media or use in a newsletter or on the internet, make sure you get the consent of the children and their parent or guardian – preferably in writing – to both taking and publishing film or photographs. Use a group picture and don't identify them by name or other personal details.

For further information and guidance contact your organisation's designated lead on safeguarding or your local authority. The Institute of Fundraising (www.institute-of-fundraising.org.uk) and the National Society for the Prevention of Cruelty to Children (www.nspcc.org.uk) also provide best practice guidance and advice.

e. Licences, certificates, consents and permits

Whatever activity you are planning, always investigate whether you require a licence.

If your venue doesn't have a licence or club premises certificate, or your particular licensable activity isn't covered under their licence, you will need to serve a Temporary Event Notice (TEN) on your local authority, environmental health and police at least 10 working days ahead of the event (England and Wales). Your event can then go ahead – possibly with some restrictions – provided there are no objections. You can also make an application for a 'late' TEN five to nine working days before the event, but this should only be done in exceptional circumstances, for example a last minute change of venue.

A TEN will cover events that involve no more than 499 people (including your staff, competitors, performers and helpers) and last up to 168 hours, or seven days. If you expect to have 500 or more people at your event at any one time, you will need to apply for a premises licence from the local authority. Bear in mind that the timescales and requirements for applying for a premises licence are significantly longer and more costly than applying for a TEN.

Licensable activity includes:

- the sale and supply of alcohol
- regulated entertainment (for instance music, singing, dancing and indoor sporting events)
- serving hot drinks and food between 11pm and 5am
- staging plays and film/video shows.

Other activities which may also require a licence, consent or permit include:

- the performance of copyrighted material and playing recorded music and videos
- door-to-door and street collections

- street trading
- fireworks
- lotteries and gambling.

If you want to sell alcohol from unlicensed premises in Scotland, you will need to apply for an occasional licence from the licensing board responsible for the area where you plan to hold your event. You may also need to apply for a separate Temporary Public Entertainment Licence and late night catering licence, as appropriate. It is advisable to give at least six weeks' notice. Contact the local licensing board for further guidance.

Licensing in Northern Ireland is more restrictive than in Great Britain and you will need to apply to the courts for a temporary licence if the premises where you want to hold your event does not have a liquor licence. Your local council will be able to provide help and advice on the application process for a temporary liquor and/or entertainment licence.

Street trading

Fundraising activities which involve selling refreshments or articles – for instance bake and plant sales, stalls at craft and summer fairs, garage and jumble sales – may require a street trading licence or consent.

A street includes any road, footway, beach or other area to which the public has access without payment. This may include doorways and entrances abutting these areas. If you have the landowner's permission and can also restrict access by charging an entry fee (which might only be a nominal 1p), it is unlikely that you will need a street trading licence or consent.

Seek advice

Whether you need a licence or consent, and what type of licence/consent, will depend on what you are doing, when and where. While there is further information about licences and consents for specific activities in the relevant sections of this guide, rules differ from one local authority to the next and fundraisers should always seek advice from their local authority or other relevant body to ensure they stay within the law.

10. How can I spread the word?

Communicate, communicate, communicate! Start publicising your event at least three months in advance. Constantly spread the word everywhere you go. Tell your neighbours, your family and friends, parents at the school gate and colleagues at your social club, gym, office or university.

Social networks like Facebook and Twitter are excellent for getting family and friends involved and can be used for regular reminders and to update people after the event.

Get your event on your charity or organisation's website, in local event calendars and in staff or community newsletters. Include a phone number and email or web address for people to find out more.

Print posters and flyers. Do you know someone with design skills who can create an eye-catching notice? Posters and leaflets will be more effective if they look professional and are in colour, rather than black and white.

Ask libraries, doctors' surgeries, leisure centres, coffee shops, hairdressers and barbers, local shops, sports clubs and parish and town councils to display them. Ask colleagues if they would put them on noticeboards at work.

Enrol family, friends and supporters to do a leaflet drop to residents in the area about two weeks before your event. Print flyers with the basic information: the time and date of the event, the main attractions, the cause or charity which will benefit and any contact information.

Send a news release to local newspapers and radio stations and ask them to cover your event. The wackier or more interesting your event or activity, the more likely it is to gain publicity.

If you can suggest a good picture and arrange a pre-event photocall, the better your chance of gaining valuable pre-event coverage.

Don't forget the smaller community newspapers and magazines, which usually have their own websites. Mention why you're raising money. If you're raising funds for a local cause or project, include what it will mean to the wider community.

Contact your local authority to see whether you can put up roadside banners and posters on roads around the venue a week or so ahead of the event. Each local authority will have its own policy, but generally they will allow limited advertising for charitable and voluntary organisations and community groups, provided notices are not unsightly or offensive and do not impact on road safety.

Remember to take posters and banners down after the event and remove any plastic ties or other fasteners.

11. Have I thanked everyone?

Tell everyone how you got on, how much you raised and how the money will be used. Thank your volunteers, your suppliers, your sponsors and the venue owner. Let everyone know how much you appreciated their support and that the event could not have taken place, or been such a success, without their help. If you've got one or two good photographs from the event put them on your organisation's website, send them to supporters and email them – with captions – to your local media.

12. How did it go?

Did you achieve your original objectives? Evaluate what worked well, what sold well, what made the most profit and what didn't work quite so well.

Ask volunteers, stallholders and contractors to fill in a feedback form so you'll know if anything needs to be changed so you can do even better next time!

2
Food and drink

We all have to eat, so why not enjoy a snack or dinner with friends and help a good cause at the same time?

Big, big breakfast

Set the day – and your fundraising – off to a scrumptious start with a bumper cooked breakfast. Offer cereals, fruit and porridge followed by bacon, sausages, eggs, beans, mushrooms, tomatoes and hash browns, washed down with copious supplies of tea and coffee. Round the meal off with toast and preserves. Do you know an inspirational speaker who would be willing to attend and entertain your guests after the meal?

Breakfast a bit too early in the day for your intended guests? How about a spot of brunch instead with eggs Benedict, scrambled eggs and smoked salmon, kedgeree or other tasty treats?

Drink coffee and eat cake

Coffee rightly deserves its status as 'liquid gold' when it comes to fundraising. Invite friends and neighbours to a coffee morning. Charge a set price or ask for donations. Make it a bit more of an occasion by serving homemade cakes and biscuits. Suggest guests bring any paperback books they've read or DVDs they've watched which you can sell to boost your funds.

Hog roast

Hog roasts are unlikely to be big fundraisers in their own right but are an ideal way to feed guests at a summer fair, barn dance or sporting event. The wonderful smell will draw people to look and eat. An average hog will take 7–10 hours to cook and will need to be regularly basted and tended to ensure the meat is tender and succulent with a crisp, golden crackling. Serve the freshly carved slices of pork with floury buns, hot sage and onion stuffing and tangy apple sauce. Provide plenty of napkins, paper plates, salt and pepper, plus an alternative for your vegetarians.

You can hire a spit and roasting equipment and buy your own hog, or pay a professional hog roast company to either roast a pig at your venue or deliver a pre-cooked and carved hog. Prices and the areas covered by hog roast caterers vary considerably, so search online for the best deal.

Seasoned cooks may feel confident to go it alone, but bear in mind that the most common food poisoning bug in Britain – campylobacter – is nicknamed the barbecue bug because it can be caught from poorly-cooked food. If you're hiring a caterer make sure the firm has a food hygiene certificate and full public and employee liability insurance.

Barbecue

Invite friends and neighbours round to a summer barbecue. Ask people who attend to pay a set admission charge. If one of your supporters has a particularly large garden, ask barbecue owners to lend their equipment – and services – and hold a mass barbecue. Provide plenty of chairs and garden tables and borrow a pop-up gazebo or two in case of rain.

Afternoon tea

Afternoon tea is a particularly British experience. It conjures up images of a bygone age – delicate bone-china cups and saucers, sandwich fingers, tiny cakes and tarts, and scones with little bowls of jam and cream, all displayed to perfection on pretty cake stands. Afternoon teas are generally held on a Saturday or Sunday afternoon – a time when your guests can unwind and relax with a partner or friends. You can hold them indoors or outside, depending on the time of year, but make sure your guests have access to toilets and hand-washing facilities.

How many people you can invite will depend on how many volunteers you can call on to help and the size of your venue. Send a formal invitation to everyone you and your helpers think might like to come, and ask them to respond by a certain date if they'd like to buy a ticket. If you've got a large venue and an army of helpers, publicise your event as widely as possible. Don't penny pinch on the table settings or the food. If you can't beg or borrow enough tablecloths, vintage crockery or cake stands, hire them in. Allow your guests between one and two hours to enjoy their tea and have waiters and waitresses on hand to check whether guests need extra tea or milk.

You could even turn your afternoon tea into a champagne tea by including a flute of bubbly in the ticket price.

Cake sale

Homemade cakes and biscuits are always a winner when it comes to fundraising. Recruit your bakers and make sure there will be a variety of cakes and cookies. Ask bakers to put a list of the ingredients with their cakes and to keep a record of how much they spent. Pay them back out of the takings. It's important that people on a limited budget don't feel unable to contribute because they can't afford the cost of the ingredients. If you're short of cakes on the day you can always top them up with shop bought cakes, but the principle of a cake sale is that the goods are homemade and people are paying extra for the creativity and effort that fundraisers have put in.

Recruit enough volunteers to sell and pack the cakes and display a big sign to make it clear who you are and what charity or cause you're supporting. If you're serving cakes in the open air, cover them with cellophane and, if rain's a possibility, take a pop-up gazebo. Encourage your bakers to be as innovative as possible. Novelty sells. Invest in making your cakes look as attractive as you can by displaying them on cake stands, in baskets and on pretty plates. Provide plates and napkins if customers are 'eating in' or bags for those who want to tuck in later.

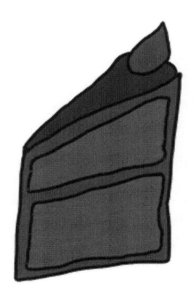

Arm yourselves with plenty of change and don't under price – better to offer discount deals such as 30p each or four for £1. If you don't manage to sell all your cakes you can always drop your prices in the last 15 minutes or see if any of your supporters are able to take them to work to sell to colleagues.

Raise extra cash with a 'guess the weight of the cake' competition, and if there's an opportunity to sell tea or coffee as well as cake – take it!

If your stall is part of a bigger event, draw attention to it by getting volunteers to wear uniforms or fancy dress. If it's getting near to Christmas, how about asking your helpers to wear Santa suits or dress as snowmen?

Charity bake off

Add an element of competition to the baking by holding a bake off. This works particularly well at workplaces, clubs and churches, where people know each other and can provide some friendly rivalry.

Decide on your categories – best fruit cake, sponge cake, tray bake, decorated cake, child's cake (under 12), etc. Provide worthwhile prizes such as kitchen or baking equipment, cash, or gift cards for stores or restaurants. Recruit a local baker, food writer or the manager at your workplace restaurant to judge the top bakes in each category. Auction off the prize-winning cakes and sell the rest for your cause. Look for additional ways to raise money. Is there an opportunity to serve hot drinks? Do you have a charity recipe book (see Compile a recipe book) or tea towels (see Create your own merchandise) you can take along to sell?

Picnic box auction

Ask your bachelors to make their idea of a romantic picnic hamper. Give each hamper a lot number and display them on tables. Present the men who made the boxes, but don't identify which one! Ask the ladies to bid for the picnic box they find most appealing and the chance to share it with the person who made it. Once all the baskets have been sold, reveal who packed which basket and leave the pair to picnic.

Teddy bears' picnic

Like most events for very young children, a teddy bears' picnic is unlikely to be a big fundraiser, but they're relatively simple to organise and a great way for pre-schools, playgroups, Sunday school classes and parent and toddler groups to have fun with their children and support a charity or good cause. You could even run the picnic as part of a bigger event such as a church or community fair or team up with other similar groups in the area for a mass picnic. Make the picnic as big or as small as you want and hold it in someone's house, a local hall, or – if you're willing to trust the weather – a garden, school playing field or local park. Send out invitations to the children, which could include a picture of a teddy or cakes which they can colour in themselves. Remind them to bring their favourite teddy. Charge a set price for tickets or ask parents to make a donation.

Recruit volunteers to help make the picnic fare – sandwiches, cocktail sausages and crisps, cherry tomatoes, teddy shaped biscuits, tiny cakes and fruit. Alternatively, you could ask people to bring their own picnic or packed lunch – which would reduce your costs and avoids catering for allergies and fussy eaters.

Keep the children entertained by singing simple nursery rhymes and playing games which they can involve their teddies in such as *Row, row, row your boat* and the *Hokey cokey*.

Dessert delight

Indulge your sweet tooth with a pudding party! One of the joys of puddings is that many of them can be cooked in advance and frozen. Everyone will have their own pudding 'party piece', whether it's a fruity pavlova, sticky chocolate pudding, lemon tart, apple pie or trifle.

Choose a date and venue and recruit a team of volunteers to make the puddings and to sell tickets before and at the event. Cut the puddings into small portions so people can get to try as many as they can manage. Provide jugs of hot custard and plenty of cream. Include a cup of tea or coffee in the ticket price or charge extra. Raise additional funds with a raffle or silent auction.

Dining for dieters

There's sure to be plenty of people in your community who are trying to lose weight. Team up with your local Weight Watchers or Slimming World consultant and ask them to help you devise a tasty meal which won't play havoc with dieters' points or 'syns'. Invite members from other groups within travelling distance of your venue to join you. Raise additional funds by holding a raffle (no chocolates!) or mini auction of pamper products and services such as manicures and beauty therapies.

Roving supper

If you've got a number of supporters who could cater for eight or more guests, why not hold a roving supper? The idea is that guests eat a starter in one home, a main dish in another and a pudding followed by tea or coffee in a third. Spread the load by recruiting volunteers to help the hosts, and make sure cooks are refunded for the cost of their course.

If you've got plenty of willing hosts and eager diners you could run a number of roving suppers at the same time. The whole group could meet in a central venue such as a village hall (perhaps for their starter) before moving on to their separate venues. Suggest people bring a bottle and have water and soft drinks available at each stop.

Make sure all the guests know how to get to their venues and give them their hosts' phone numbers in case they get lost. You could add to the enjoyment by setting a theme for the evening and suggesting guests dress accordingly.

Fundraising dinner

A fundraising dinner, or dinner dance, can take whatever form you like, from a formal meal in a top hotel to a buffet and barn dance in your local church or community hall. What you choose to do, and where you choose to do it, will depend on how much you think your guests will be willing to pay and whether you can attract high net worth individuals or local businesses and groups to buy tables at the event. Allow plenty of time to book a venue and to promote the event.

Check out venues such as golf, sailing and sports clubs, as well as hotels. It's likely that your venue will want to provide the food. Ask if they are able to offer a discount for a charity event, and work with their caterers to find a menu which is both appetising and good value.

Most fundraising dinners will also include some sort of entertainment for the guests, such as singers, musicians, a comedian, an entertaining speaker or some form of dancing.

Send out invitations to as many people as you can, especially family and friends and local businesses and groups connected to your cause or that might be interested in helping your cause.

Make sure you charge enough for tickets to cover all your expenses and make a good return on your hard work. Raise additional funds with a raffle, auction or other activity at the event.

Host your own dinner party

Make it as formal or informal, as big or as small as you want. Why not pick a theme and ask guests to dress in clothes from the 1960s or 1970s and play appropriate background music, or to come as sci-fi goodies and baddies? Check whether your guests have any dietary requirements or allergies, and charge a set price or ask for donations.

Tapas and sangria

A menu of Spanish small plates teamed with refreshing sangria is a perfect fundraiser for summer evenings. The tapas pack plenty of flavour without being too filling or time-consuming to make. Many of the dishes can be cooked ahead – for instance olives can be left to gently marinate for up to a month before the big day.

Sangria is basically wine punch made from Rioja or other Spanish red with fruits such as berries, apples and oranges. Add orange juice or other sweetener, sparkling lemonade and a small amount of brandy, whisky or orange-flavoured liqueur (which can be omitted if you want to reduce the alcohol content). There's also a 'blanca' version made from white wine with melon and tangerines.

A tapas and sangria party can be a sit-down affair or an opportunity for people to eat and socialise on their feet. The more guests you have, the greater the variety of tapas you can prepare. Plan a menu that enables you to offer a good selection of flavours with plenty of choice for vegetarians. Ask each of your chefs to cook large quantities of particular tapas and divide them into small dishes. Easy-to-cook favourites include stuffed and marinated olives, stuffed tomatoes, griddled or roasted Mediterranean vegetables, prawns in garlic butter, croquettes filled with Serrano ham, spicy meatballs and paella.

Decorate the tables with bright tablecloths and napkins, colourful pottery and fresh flowers.

Make sure you've got enough small plates and glasses. Set the mood with background music or book a flamenco guitarist or singer – and charge accordingly!

International evening

If you're fundraising to visit another country, organise an evening with food, drinks and entertainment from the area you plan to visit. Dress your volunteers in the country's national dress and decorate the room to tie in with your theme. Or simply host an Indian, Italian, Caribbean or other 'world meal' at your home for friends and family. Ask everyone to dress up and charge them a set price, or ask them to make a donation to your cause.

Organise a night out at a local pub or restaurant

Approach your local restaurants, pubs and pizzerias to see if they would be willing to host a fundraiser at their premises. Negotiate a deal, particularly if you're willing to book when they're less busy mid-week, and charge a set price for a ticket.

Fortune cookies

A fortune cookie is a crisp, triangular shell made from eggs, flour, corn starch, vanilla, sugar and milk or water. Hidden inside is a small strip of paper with words of wisdom, a proverb or 'prediction'. Don't worry about baking them; there are plenty of companies which will make them for you in small or large quantities. The message inside can be general or personalised to suit your event or cause.

You could also use them as tombola 'tickets'. People buy a cookie, a certain number of which contain a message awarding a prize. Anyone who doesn't win a prize still gets the cookie (see Lotteries and non-commercial gaming and betting).

Popcorn and candy floss – all the fun of the fair

Freshly cooked popcorn and candy floss are very popular, especially with young adults and children. They're also extremely profitable. The popcorn ingredients – vegetable oil, sugar or salt, and corn – and a box or cone to serve it in, will cost around 19p a portion but sell for £1 or £1.50. It's the same with candy floss, which is simply sugar which has been heated and then spun very fast. One 2kg bag of granulated sugar will produce about 100 servings, which once you've added the cost of powdered food colouring and a stick or cone, works out at around 6p each.

You can hire or buy commercial popcorn and candy floss makers and all the ingredients you'll need online. Shop around to get the best deal. If you hold regular events, your machine will pay for itself very quickly. You can make it work even harder by hiring it out (with or without an operator) to other groups to use at school fairs, movie shows, sports days and other events.

If you're not sure whether it's worth investing in a machine, test the market by hiring a machine or, for popcorn, buy in bulk online and see how it sells. A 3kg bag of popcorn with enough for 60–80 portions will cost around £30 and you'll only need to add the cost of boxes or cones.

Tuck shop

Buy different sweets in bulk and pack them in cones made from coloured paper or cellophane wrap. Tie the sweets and wrappings in with any theme you're using. The idea is to make them look as attractive as possible. Make bunches of flowers from small, coloured lollipops, twist green paper 'leaves' around the outside and secure with sticky tape. Sell them at work or school, at fairs, car boot sales (if their terms and conditions permit) and other events.

Eating competitions

Not quite the Egon Ronay of fundraising, but some people have an appetite for this kind of thing. The challenge is to see who can eat the most – cornflakes, cream crackers, loaves of bread or whatever other delicacy you choose – within a set time. Or how about eating jelly with chopsticks?

Ask contestants to raise money through sponsorship and charge friends and relatives an entrance fee to watch. Sell refreshments (which should be far more appetising than the competitors' fare!).

Cheese and wine party

Find a cheese connoisseur or enthusiast who can talk about the different cheeses. If there's a delicatessen near you, they may be willing to help run the event and bring a selection of cheeses to sell on the night. Make sure you have a spread of really good cheeses. Include some unusual ones – particularly any made locally – that people might not have sampled before, and provide a selection of biscuits. Select wines to complement the cheeses and serve them in nice glasses. Don't stint on quality – and set your ticket price accordingly.

Wine tasting

Wine tastings give your guests an opportunity to not only sample wines they might not have tried before, but also to socialise with friends and find out more about your charity or cause.

Many people enjoy wine but few claim to be wine connoisseurs – and those who do are likely to go to more professional wine tastings – so place the emphasis on organising a light-hearted social event.

You may already know of a knowledgeable and personable wine expert who would be willing to choose and talk about the wines. If not, find a sommelier or wine merchant who can also supply suitable wines. Give your wine expert an idea of the type of people likely to attend your event so they can gauge the variety and price of the wines to taste. Negotiate on price – you're giving them the opportunity to win new customers and additional sales on the night, as well as promoting their business when you publicise the event.

You'll need a venue with tables and chairs, catering facilities and a fridge or large container with ice for wines that need to be served chilled. Ask your expert for advice on what type of canapés or other light refreshments to serve to complement the wines, and to provide a short description of each wine for people to take away.

Appoint a master of ceremonies to welcome the guests, introduce your wine expert and explain what will be happening.

Charge for tickets and add other fundraising activities such as a silent auction, raffle or tombola. Negotiate a commission on any orders taken on the night or, if your licence allows, any bottles sold at the event.

Beer tasting

There are hundreds of different beers, from the bitter yet floral flavours of a strong blonde ale to a dark ale or stout. Beer tastings are generally hosted by a local brewery, but you could ask your brewer if they would come to your venue. Decide how many guests you can comfortably cater for and how much you'll serve of each beer.

Beer and food have gone together since the days when water was undrinkable and ale was served instead. Provide light refreshments which will complement the beers – perhaps a sweet and spicy pickle with blonde ale, the saltiness of prawns with sour beer or the coriander flavours in Indian food with wheat beer. Make sure you've plenty of tables and chairs, catering facilities, a fridge or ice for beers that need to be kept cool and good quality glasses.

Let guests know in advance what sort of food you'll be serving so, if you're only serving appetisers or light bites, they can have something to eat before they go out and aren't drinking on an empty stomach.

Cider tasting

Instead of beer, why not hold a cider tasting? The UK has the highest consumption per head of cider in the world. Contact a local cider brewery or a pub which specialises in cider, with a view to them hosting the event or coming to your venue. Decide on the range of ciders to sample, from the sweet to the dry and some of the perry (pear) or newer berry ciders, as well as how much of each to serve. Ask your expert to provide tasting notes, and serve a hearty ploughman's lunch, hot pasty and crisps or pie and mash.

Cocktail party

The beauty of a cocktail party – apart from the eye-catching colour of the drinks – is the vast array available. And that's the big headache for anyone organising a cocktail party fundraiser. Do you offer a wide variety of cocktails – and risk having costly spirits, liqueurs and other ingredients left over – or restrict the choice to prosecco-, rum-, or vodka-based drinks?

A solution might be to ask a local pub or hotel to run the cocktail bar for you, either at your venue or in a room at their premises. Decide how many cocktails you want to serve each guest and whether you will be offering a variety of samples or a smaller number of larger cocktails. Ambiance is everything, so set the mood with the decorations and music. Put bowls of crisps, olives and nuts on the tables and serve bite-size refreshments to complement the cocktails. End the evening by serving tea and coffee with chocolates or petits fours.

***

Alcohol (liquor) licensing

If you're planning to sell or serve alcohol at your event, check whether your venue has a premises licence or club premises certificate which includes the sale of alcohol. You will need to check the conditions on the licence and whether or not there are any restrictions.

If your venue doesn't have a licence or certificate to sell alcohol, or if the licence doesn't meet your requirements, you'll need to serve a Temporary Event Notice (TEN) on the local authority, police and environmental health, at least 10 working days before your event (England and Wales). There is also provision to serve a short notice TEN (five to nine working days prior to the event), but this should only be used when unforeseen circumstances, such as a last minute change of venue, lead to short notice. The TEN can cover the supply and sale of alcohol as well as various types of regulated entertainment, such as live or recorded music, and the supply of hot food and drink between 11pm and 5am. You will also need a TEN if any activity you want to run is not included within the terms of the venue's licence.

The premises user under the TEN will be responsible for the sale and/or provision of alcohol and any other activities under the TEN and may be liable if there are any breaches.

You will need to obtain an occasional (temporary) licence from the local licensing board if you plan to sell alcohol from unlicensed premises in

Scotland. If you're planning to sell alcohol in Northern Ireland and the premises where you want to hold your event do not have a liquor licence, you will need to apply to the courts for an occasional licence. Contact the local council for guidance.

If alcohol is included in the ticket price, or if you ask guests to make a donation in return for an alcoholic drink, this is classed as sale of alcohol, and you will need a licence. Make sure your bar staff are aware of the restrictions on selling alcohol and display a price list so people know how many millilitres their glass of wine or beer will contain. As an alternative, why not provide glasses and invite guests to bring a bottle and charge a suitable corkage fee?

Some supermarkets allow you to borrow trays of glasses and most will refund you for any unopened bottles you have purchased from their store.

A successful event is one where everyone gets home safely. Provide plenty of soft drinks and water so non-drinkers don't feel left out and those drinking alcohol keep hydrated. Keep an eye on your guests to make sure no-one's drinking is getting out of hand and have a list of nearby taxi companies handy. If you're organising a beer tasting or similar event involving alcohol, consider appointing volunteers as designated drivers or hire a mini bus and driver to pick up and drop people off for an additional charge.

***

Food safety

Any food which is being sold or supplied at your event must comply with food safety regulations. Food which is sold for a charity or community organisation (jams, cakes, etc) or at one-off events such as community fun days, won't need to be labelled unless the charity or organisation is a registered food business. Even if you're not legally required to label a food, it's good practice to label the item with the name of the product and a list of ingredients (in descending order of weight), particularly common allergens such as peanuts and tree nuts (walnuts, almonds, etc), gluten, eggs, soybeans and milk. Make sure the information you provide is clear and accurate.

The Food Standards Agency (www.food.gov.uk) provides catering advice for charity and community groups on preparing, handling, transporting and serving food.

Your local authority environmental health or trading standards department will also be able to advise you about any regulations which would apply to your particular event. If you're using a caterer, ask to see their food hygiene certificate and public and employer's liability insurance before you sign the contract.

***

See also: How do I make it safe and legal?; Licensing – playing live and recorded music; Auctions and Lotteries and non-commercial gaming and betting.

3
Music, movies and dancing

Staging any kind of musical event is a great way to raise funds. Your success is guaranteed if you can persuade a 'big name' singer, orchestra or band to perform, but smaller events starring local bands or choirs are just as enjoyable and can be very profitable.

Your theme will be influenced by your choice of music and musicians, venue, and times of year and day. Will it be jazz in the park with picnic hampers, a candlelight concert with wine in the local church or a pianist tinkling on the ivories accompanied by afternoon tea? Whatever you choose, whether it be a string quartet, choir or band, think about who will be interested in coming and what time is most suitable for them.

First of all find a band or group that is willing to perform, ideally for a reduced fee or even on an expenses-only basis. Your chances of attracting a well-known performer will depend largely on your contacts and those of your charity and supporters. Does anyone have a friend or relation in the music industry, or who runs or works in a music venue, who can help you by approaching the

performers on your behalf or by giving you contact details for them or their agent?

Bear in mind that Friday and Saturday evenings are the busiest times for performers and you may need to book well in advance. If your contacts fail to turn up trumps, scour local newspapers and search online to see who's performing where and when and contact any performers you think might be suitable. If you are fundraising for a musical society, church or school, finding people to perform may be easier.

Sell tickets as early as possible to fill your venue and cover your costs. Consider offering an 'early bird' discount to people who buy their tickets by a certain date or a discount to people who buy 10 or more tickets.

Allow your musicians plenty of time to set up and test their equipment. Ask them whether they are bringing, or will need, a stage. Reserve a parking space for them as near to the venue as possible as they will need to move heavy pieces of equipment and instruments in and out. Ask how they would like to be paid – some will prefer to be paid in cash so they can split it up between themselves at the end of the evening.

Hold an 'open mic' night

An open mic is a live show where members of the audience can get 10–15 minutes at the microphone to play music, sing, read a poem – which they may have written themselves – tell a few jokes, act a scene from a play, etc.

Get as many people as possible who are willing to perform signed up in advance. You may want to set rules such as maximum length of time at the mic and no swearing or crudity, particularly if there will be children in the audience. Check whether they will need any extra equipment and give them a time slot.

You'll need a good compère who will set the tone and atmosphere for the event, introduce the acts, encourage people to take part on the night and make sure the show runs on time. Decide if you want to include refreshments in the ticket price and, if so, whether you want to serve food before the performances, or during the interval.

Talent show

Hold a talent show and give would-be stars a chance to shine. You'll be surprised at the hidden talent that exists in your club, church congregation, school or workplace. Organising a talent show or talent competition is very similar to running an open mic event.

First, decide what style of acts you want for your show, whether you just want musicians and singers, or if you're happy to embrace actors, comedians, dancers, magicians, etc.

Try to attract as many acts as you can – the more performers, the more friends and relatives will attend. If possible, hold auditions, particularly if you have too many potential performers, and check their material is suitable for your target audience.

Set out a few basic rules, such as performance time, and whether people can perform as an individual, and then again in a duet or group. Check whether they need you to provide any equipment for their act, for example a table or chair, and what equipment, if any, they will be bringing with them.

If you want to run it as a competition, think about whether you want the audience to vote for their top act, to appoint a judge, or – if you are showcasing a wide range of expertise – a panel of judges.

Look for a friendly, approachable and unflappable compère who will be able to introduce and talk about the various acts as they come on and leave the stage and cope with any problems – from stage fright to acts running late – that occur during the event.

Charge an admission fee, which could include a light snack. Sell advertising space in the programme and run other fundraising activities on the night.

Battle of the bands

If you want to hold a battle of the bands, you'll need to find enough bands to battle it out. Think about whether you want a particular type of music – rock, jazz, classical, folk, etc or a variety. Ask your supporters if they know of any up-and-coming or wannabee bands and advertise for bands that meet your criteria. Try Student Union bars, musical societies, recording studios, church music groups, schools and local pubs. Contact the music critic of your local newspaper to see if they can suggest potential contenders.

It's a good idea to hold auditions to ensure the bands are up to a high enough standard and to check their material is suitable for your audience.

Once you've got your search for bands underway, start thinking about your 'battleground'. Will it be a local pub, church, school hall or sports club? Be realistic about how many people you will be able to attract – there's nothing more dispiriting for performers than playing to a handful of people in a vast auditorium. Does the venue have the type of atmosphere that's right for your genre of music? Is it suitable for hosting live music, with good acoustics and plenty of plug sockets for the various instruments and equipment?

Check whether your bands will be bringing their own sound and lighting equipment and technician or if they are expecting you to provide equipment or technical support.

Decide what prize you want to award to the winning band and how to decide the victors. Do you want the audience to vote for their favourite act or do you want to bring in an outside judge or panel? If you don't know anyone in the music industry who might be willing to judge, see if the music critic at your local paper or a local radio DJ would be willing to help.

Consider whether you will charge the bands an entry fee, ask them to perform for nothing or offer to pay reasonable expenses. Sell tickets and run your own bar or, if you're using licensed premises, ask your venue if they would donate a percentage of their takings. Invite businesses and local bands to advertise in the event programme. Serve refreshments and run other fundraising activities.

Hymnathon

How about a hymnathon, particularly if you're fundraising for a church? This could take various forms. You could set yourselves the challenge of singing through the entire *New English Hymnal* or other book without a break, or singing as many hymns as possible within a set time.

Don't try to go it alone unless you have a large congregation and an enormous music group. Take the opportunity to bring people into your church and build community by asking local choirs of every kind and affiliation, of all faiths and none, to sing in half- or one-hour slots.

Make sure you get plenty of publicity for the hymnathon, and put banners outside the church or other venue. Post someone outside the door to encourage passers-by who hear the singing to pop inside to listen or to join in.

Invite individuals, businesses and organisations to sponsor an individual, choir or particular hymn. Sell programmes listing the hymns, sponsors and choirs at the door. Sell teas, coffees and light refreshments before, during and after the event. If you're running a buy-a-brick fundraiser or have merchandise to sell, sell it. Think about any other fundraising activities which you could add such as a cake or plant sale or craft or book stall.

Karaoke party

Decide where you want to hold your karaoke party – at your own or a supporter's home, at work, in a room at a local pub or at a community hall.

Add to the occasion by having a theme for the party – for instance hits from the stage and screen or pop music from the '70s or '80s. Tie your décor into the theme – put up posters, beg or borrow the odd mirror ball and see if it's possible to replace plain light bulbs with coloured ones. Design your publicity materials to complement your theme and encourage guests to dress the part.

There's a huge variety of karaoke machines available. Whichever is best for you will depend on your venue and how many people you think will come. Ask around to see if you can borrow or hire a machine and make sure you check that it works and is loud enough for your needs.

Karaoke is thirsty work so provide plenty of liquid refreshment. Keep any food light. If you've decided a theme for the party carry it through to the food. If you're belting out *Maggie May*, *Highway to Hell* and *Stayin' Alive* from the '70s, then serve up mini prawn cocktails in shot glasses, cheese and pineapple or silverskin onions on sticks, vol-au-vents, chicken drumsticks and Black Forest gateau.

Appoint a compère or host to tell everyone a bit about your charity or good cause, take requests from guests, encourage everyone to take a turn at the microphone and keep order.

Award joke prizes (which tie in with your theme) for the best male and female singers and best costumes. Charge for tickets and add other fundraising activities.

Movie night

Everyone loves a good movie and a film night fundraiser is a great way to build community. Why not transform your venue into a cinema for an evening or matinee performance? Film events can be quick and easy to organise; you just need to make sure you've got the appropriate licences.

What movie to show? First of all, think about the age of your audience. If you want an all-age screening, ensure the film is appropriate for everyone in the audience. The age of your audience will also determine the timing of your screening.

Why not go to town and include the film as part of a themed event? Will it be romance, mystery, horror, gangsters, spies, sci-fi or comic book heroes? Encourage your guests to dress to fit the theme, challenge them with a movie quiz, and serve hot and cold drinks, popcorn, hot dogs and ice cream.

All commercially distributed films are subject to copyright. This means you will need a Single Title Screening Licence (STSL) if you plan to show a movie for money. The licence can be obtained direct from Filmbank Distributors Ltd (see Useful contacts and resources) and will enable you to advertise your event and charge a ticket fee. You will need to pay a deposit to open an account and a minimum of £83 per title per screening or 35% of the ticket sales – whichever is the greater. Filmbank can supply the DVD to you or you can book the licence only and use your own DVD copy of the film. You, or your venue, will also need PRS for Music and Phonographic Performance Limited (PPL) licences to cover the soundtrack (see Useful contacts and resources for contact details).

If your venue is not licensed to show films you will also need to serve a Temporary Event Notice (TEN) on the local authority.

One of the benefits of the STSL is that some films are available through Filmbank three to four months after cinema release and before they are released on DVD, providing an opportunity for you to stage your very own premiere, complete with red carpet and 'celebrity' dinner.

Raise funds through ticket sales and refreshments, and add a silent auction or raffle. (If refreshments are included in the ticket price, deduct their value when reporting ticket sales to Filmbank.)

Dancing

Barn dancing, line dancing, zumba, ballroom or disco – take your pick. You'll need to find a venue that's big enough to take everyone dancing at the same time, with a good dance floor which is smooth but not slippery and has nothing which would cause any dancers to stumble.

Unless you are fundraising for a dance group or society, it is unlikely that all of your potential participants will know the steps or feel sufficiently confident to take to the floor. This means you'll need to appoint or employ a dance instructor to explain the steps to beginners and to help select suitable music. Appoint a master of ceremonies who can introduce your instructor and explain what will be happening and when.

If you are using a live band rather than recorded music, ask them if they want a stage. Have tables and chairs available for those who want to take a break from dancing, and choose food which can be served and eaten quickly so people don't lose valuable dancing time.

Make the dress code clear in the invitation – loose clothing and comfortable shoes or something more formal?

Barn dance

A barn dance, or English ceilidh, is ideal for people of all ages and fitness levels, needs no prior knowledge or experience and is something that a whole community can do and enjoy together.

The emphasis is on having a good time and not taking things too seriously. Barn dances are social events, so allow 15 minutes or so for people to catch up with friends before starting the dancing.

Appoint or employ a 'caller' or instructor, who will explain and teach the various dances using standard formations such as circles, squares and lines. Once the dancing starts in earnest, the caller will shout out reminders of the steps to the dancers. Finding the right caller is important – ask around for recommendations and see if you can watch them in action at another event.

Check that your venue is big enough for all your dancers to be in a circle with their arms outstretched. If you're having a bar, try not to put it in another room, or you run the risk that people will end up there instead of on the dance floor. Provide some seating around the floor – bales of hay would be a nice touch – so people can take a break if they get tired.

How long the dancers spend on the floor will depend on how fit they are, but you'll achieve a good balance if you aim for two and a half to three hours of dancing with an interval for some form of refreshment after the first hour or hour and a half.

The caller will normally provide their own recorded music, but if your budget stretches to a live band, they will probably want a stage so they, and the caller, can see the dancers.

Sell tickets before the event and at the door.

Disco

Discos are probably the easiest form of dancing to organise and work particularly well as school and youth group fundraisers. Allow four to six weeks to plan and promote your disco. Hire a DJ who can play a wide variety of music to suit different tastes and check that they have their own public liability insurance cover. Give the disco a theme – for instance a summer, Valentine's Day or Christmas disco – and decorate the room accordingly.

Discos are relatively cheap to run, which means you can keep the ticket price quite low. Decide whether you want to sell tickets on the night or adopt a ticket-only policy. Fundraise by providing a bar (if the disco is for adults) and refreshments. If your disco is mainly for young people, sell glow sticks, hot dogs, sweets and soft drinks. Make sure parents are aware that there'll be treats to buy so children bring some pocket money.

***

Licensing – live and recorded music

You will generally need a licence if an event involves public entertainment such as live or recorded music, dancing, plays and film or video shows.

Alcohol licensed premises and venues such as church and village halls, community premises and schools and colleges – which are classed as workplaces under the Live Music Act – don't need a licence for amplified live music between 8am and 11pm provided there are fewer than 200 people attending. You won't need a licence to put on unamplified live music between the same hours and there is no limit on the size of the audience unless it's taking place on licensed premises. If your music is amplified, and you expect to have 200 or more people at your event, you will need to serve a Temporary Event Notice (England and Wales) on the local authority, environmental health and police.

If you want to hold your event at licensed premises, check that the activities you want to carry out, and when you want to hold the event, are covered by their licence/club premises certificate. If they're not, you may need to serve a TEN.

The Live Music Act doesn't apply in Scotland or Northern Ireland, where you will need to apply for a temporary public entertainment licence – your local authority will be able to give you further help and guidance.

The government is planning to relax the requirements for community events such as the showing of a film, a live music performance and any playing of recorded music. Check with your local authority to make sure you are getting the most up-to-date information.

If you are using a live band or music that is copyright protected, you will need to check that the venue has a PRS for Music licence. If you are playing recorded music or music videos – including movies – your venue will also need to have a Phonographic Performance Limited (PPL) licence. PRS and PPL ensure that royalties are distributed to the creators of the work, the performers, publishers and record companies. They are separate companies, represent different rights holders and have different terms and conditions. If your venue does not have a PRS or PPL licence, you will need to contact either, or both, organisations (see Useful contacts and resources).

***

See also: How do I make it safe and legal?; Alcohol (liquor) licensing and Food safety.

4
Shows and fairs

Organising larger fundraising events can pay off big time as they not only have the potential to raise substantial amounts of money, but by involving the wider community, will make more people aware of your charity or cause.

Wedding dress display

You'd be surprised at how many women have still got their wedding dresses in a box in the loft, vacuum packed and under the bed or hanging in a wardrobe, treasured but unseen. Why not give them an outing for charity? You'll collect so many stories along with the dresses, that gaining media coverage will be a cinch.

Ask married ladies living in the community if they'd loan their wedding dresses for an exhibition. Cover as many generations as you can – those who have just tied the knot and others who have been married for 20, 40, 60 or even more years, to show how designs and fabrics have changed over the years.

Approach local fashion stores to see if they would be willing to lend or donate mannequins or display busts. Some of your contributors may have kept not only their dresses but also the shoes, veils, tiaras and headdresses worn on their wedding day. Display the dresses – designer, off-the-peg or homemade – the bigger the variety the better – alongside framed photographs of the bride and groom and stories from their special day or how they met. Decorate the church or other venue with flowers. The dresses and memorabilia will be precious to those who have loaned them, so make sure there are sufficient people on duty when the exhibition is open and that the venue is secured whenever it's not staffed. Check out the insurance details in case anything gets damaged or lost and make sure the owners are clear as to who will bear the risk if there are any problems.

Raise funds by charging an admission fee and offer advertising space at your venue and in the programme to wedding services providers. Sell refreshments, which could include slices of wedding cake, and wedding 'favours' – small paper cones or pots of sweets.

Flower festival

Some of the bigger flower festivals run by large churches and cathedrals will take a year or so to prepare but can draw many thousands of visitors. But a flower festival doesn't have to be big to be beautiful! Pick a theme for your festival such as 'the creation of the world' or 'earth and air'. Hire professional floral art designers to provide the exhibits or invite arrangers from local flower arrangement clubs and churches to enter a display. Secure a small panel of judges and award prizes for the top arrangements in different categories, for example best pedestal arrangement or best use of accessories.

Raise money at your festival by selling admission programmes. Seek sponsorship for the event and for individual categories, and sell advertising space in the programme and at the venue. Serve refreshments and consider adding craft and plant stalls. Could you arrange an evening concert or choral event in the venue during the festival?

Christmas tree festival

A Christmas tree festival is a wonderful way to start the countdown to Christmas. Ask local businesses, clubs and families if they'd like to provide and decorate a Christmas tree, either as part of an overall theme or to their own design. It's a lovely opportunity for people to show support for their local community and portray their group or organisation in an imaginative way, perhaps by decorating their tree in their corporate colours or with decorations based on their products or services.

Christmas tree festivals tend to be held in early December and run for anything from 2–10 days. Look for a large church, hall or other building with room for at least 20–30 trees. Set some basic rules to include the maximum height and width of trees – which could be real, artificial or one-off designs. Put a notice by each tree saying who has decorated it and the theme or title of their exhibit. You could even add a bit of competition by asking visitors to vote for their favourite tree.

Invite people to wander through the forest of glittering trees. Make a small charge, set a higher entrance fee to include a hot drink and a mince pie or simply invite visitors to make a donation. Add to the festive atmosphere with live or recorded music and seasonal goodies.

Make the most of the wonderful sight of a darkened room or building filled by the glow from hundreds of fairy lights, by holding an evening concert during the festival.

Why not run a Christmas craft stall during the festival, sell your branded merchandise (see Create your own merchandise) or run special activities for children such as story readings or a competition to draw and decorate their own Christmas tree?

Fashion show

Give your supporters the chance to sashay down the catwalk in a charity fashion show. These work particularly well in schools and clubs and provide a talking point for people for weeks before and after the event.

A fashion show can take a number of different forms. You can arrange and manage it yourself, or employ a company which will run the event for you. In either case you'll need a hall with room for racks of clothing and tables to display accessories for people to browse through. You'll also need suitable staging or a central area for your catwalk, seating for your audience and nearby rooms with full-length mirrors where your models can get changed and have their hair and make-up done (approach local hairdressers and beauticians to see if they would provide their services free or for a reduced fee). The rooms can be used at the end of the show for people to try on anything that caught their eye. You'll also need a PA system for your compère and suitable music to accompany the models down the catwalk.

Ask local fashion retailers if they would be willing to have their clothes or accessories included in the fashion parade. Some department stores may be willing to stage the entire show for you. Negotiate a commission for anything they sell and ask them to promote and advertise your fashion show in their shop. There's something in it for them as well as you. They'll be seen to be supporting their local community, gain publicity and get the opportunity to sell their clothes at your event.

If you don't feel up to organising the event yourself, there are a number of companies which specialise in running fashion shows. These companies will generally provide the clothes, display racks, tills and card machines, PA, compère and models (unless you have people desperate to get on the catwalk!) and anything else you might need. This means you can focus on providing the venue, publicising the show, selling tickets and providing refreshments. The companies make their money from selling clothes at the event and will also offer you a commission on everything they sell.

Charge an entrance fee and sell advertising space in the event programme. Sell drinks and other refreshments on the night and add a raffle or silent auction.

Fun dog show

Every dog has its day – and this could be your pet's turn! Dog shows are a great way for dog owners and dog lovers to get together, show off their pets, have some fun and raise money.

Fun dog shows can be run as part of a bigger event, such as a summer fair or as the main activity. A quick search on the internet will find plenty of veterinary groups and dog magazines offering advice and practical help to set up a dog show. The best sites will help you with publicity by registering your show in their calendar of events, enabling dog lovers to search for the dates and locations of local  shows. They will also offer suggestions for gaining sponsorship, give ideas for classes and generate templates for entry forms, posters, programmes, judging sheets and winners' certificates.

It's important to ensure the safety and well-being of people and animals. Provide plenty of water and dog bowls, poop disposal bags and bins, and require owners to keep their animals on leads or in pet carriers unless they're on stage or participating in an event. Ask your local pet shops and vets to display posters advertising the event and keep a stock of flyers to hand out to dog owners and walkers.

Make your money by charging an entry fee for each class. Ask pet food companies, pet shops and veterinary practices if they would be willing to advertise in your event programme, sponsor a class and/or provide prizes. Serve refreshments and add other fundraising activities such as stalls selling dog-related items, a raffle, tombola and games such as 'lucky collar' (hoopla) or guess the weight of the dog.

Pet show

A pet show will draw pet owners and pet lovers from around your community. First decide what pets you want to include. Do you want to restrict it to pets of a particular species or size? Are snakes and pet pigs, cats and dogs welcome or do you want to restrict it to the smaller pets such as rabbits, mice, guinea pigs, hamsters, stick insects, snails or even a tarantula or two?

Your choice of location will be a determining factor – some venues may not allow pets. Think about what time of year you want to hold your show. If you decide to have your show outside, beware of the weather. Temperatures can become  unbearably hot or rain can turn fields into quagmires. Do you know a vet who could attend and give advice on pet care?

There's plenty of advice and material online if you search for 'running a pet show'. A number of veterinary practices or groups will offer ideas for categories, sponsorship, prizes and setting rules as well as templates for entry forms, publicity material and marking forms for judges. Advertise your show in local schools, shops – particularly pet shops – and veterinary practices.

It's essential to ensure the safety and welfare of people and pets. Have plenty of water on hand as well as supplies to clean up after the animals. Raise money by charging for admission, providing refreshments and adding other fundraisers, particularly pet related, activities – such as splat the rat or hook a duck (see Fairs and fun days).

Fairs and fun days

School, church or community fun days and fairs have been the backbone of community fundraising for generations. They're big money spinners and great fun for everyone but need plenty of planning and a committed team. Recruit a steering group to oversee the event and allocate responsibilities such as recruiting and co-ordinating volunteers, publicity, finance, sponsorship, etc. School Parent Teacher Associations (PTAs) in particular have plenty of experience of running summer fairs and you'll find excellent advice and checklists on running a fair together with ideas for stalls and entertainment on PTA websites.

Choose your entertainment so there's something for everyone. Think about a crowd puller like a tribute band, falconry display, circus act, etc. Do you, or any of your supporters, have a connection with a well-known actor, singer or sports person who you could approach to open the event? A 'top name' will draw more people and the fact they're turning out to support your event or cause will give a boost to your publicity.

Are there any local choirs, church music groups, brass bands or jazz bands that would be willing to perform in support of their community or your cause in return for their expenses or a small fee? Are there local martial arts, cheerleader, belly dancing, fencing, acrobatic or gymnastic groups who would be proud to display their skills?

Children in particular love small animals. Is there a local pet shop or animal sanctuary that would bring their furry or feathered friends? Do you have enough space to include a mini dog show? How about a bouncy castle, fun fair ride, Punch and Judy show and face painting?

Decide whether you want to invite other charities and community groups to have a stall or display at your event. Aim for a good variety of stalls – crafts, plants, bric-a-brac, etc – so there's something for everyone. Invite the local ice cream vendor to attend – and charge an appropriate price for the pitch. Don't forget those all important homemade cakes, cream teas, drinks and other refreshments, which are guaranteed to make you a profit.

Provide plenty of activities for adults and children – fun days and fairs are fundraising's equivalent of pick and mix. It doesn't matter if some of them are free or only raise a few pounds. If people are having a good time they'll stay longer and be more likely to return next year (perhaps with more money to spend). By drawing (and keeping) a crowd, you'll also attract even more people to your event as passers-by pop in to find out what's going on.

Tried and tested activities, like these below, will add to the fun as well as your funds. Remember to do a risk assessment for each activity as well as the event itself. You don't want anyone to be hit by a flying boot, stray ball or piece of crockery.

- **Splat the rat.** Attach a length of drainpipe to a plank which is slightly longer than the pipe. The rats are made from bean bags with whiskers, a tail and little faces, which are heavy enough to drop smoothly – and quickly – down the pipe. The rats are dropped down the pipe and contestants have to use a stick to try and pin the rat against the board as it drops out of the tube.
- **Welly wanging.** Competitors throw a wellington boot as far as they can down a course. Award a prize to the man, woman and child who is top welly wanger in their category. As an alternative, challenge players to wang their welly into a laundry basket and award a prize to those who do.
- **Ball in a bucket.** Competitors throw a ball and win a prize if it lands in the bucket.
- **Darts.** Award a prize for the highest scoring man, woman or child or small spot prizes to anyone who scores a bull's eye.
- **Test your strength.** Hire or buy a machine – it's a game you can wheel out time and time again. The aim is to hit the base unit as hard as you can with a mallet to force an object upward to record the strength of the blow or, if the blow is powerful enough, to ring a bell.
- **Raffle.** (See Lotteries and non-commercial gaming and betting.)
- **Tombola.** (See Lotteries and non-commercial gaming and betting.)
- **Silent auction.**
- **Guess the weight of the cake or number of sweets in a jar.** The nearest guess wins the item.
- **Coconut shy.** You'll need between three and five metal coconut holders, a supply of wooden balls and plenty of coconuts. Set the shy up against a wire fence or a backdrop made from tarpaulin or old blankets to absorb the impact from the balls.
- **Roll a penny.** The penny, or other coin, must land on a playing card or other marker to win a prize.
- **Lucky dip.** There's a prize every time, which makes this a must for any event involving young children. Wrap small prizes in paper – newspaper will do – and place them in a tub of polystyrene chips.

- **Hoopla.** Mount your prizes (soft toys, sweets, bottles of wine, toiletries, etc) on wooden blocks. Traditionally, the hoop must clear the prize and all four corners of the block to win. This is very difficult, so you may wish to set your own rules as to what constitutes a winning throw. Bear in mind that under licensing laws anyone under 18 cannot be given alcohol as a prize.
- **Hook a duck.** Float plastic ducks with eyelets on their heads and numbers on their bottoms in a child's paddling pool. Players pay to hook a duck out of the water with each number corresponding to a prize.
- **Tin can alley.** Remove the back from an old book shelf and stack empty food cans in pyramids of three, six, etc. Arm your competitors with water guns or wet foam pads and award prizes depending on how many they manage to knock off the shelf.
- **Crockery smash.** Put out a call for old and chipped crockery. Pile the crockery on a table or display unit on heavy duty polythene or dust sheets. Charge people for three hard balls and the opportunity to smash as much crockery as they can.
- **Lucky lollies.** Paint the bottom part of some lolly sticks and stick them all in sand or foam. If the contestant picks a lolly with a coloured stick they win the lolly or a small prize. Other variations of the game include **prickly hedgehog** (use cocktail sticks in a paper mache or foam hedgehog) and **lucky straws** (push a piece of paper down each straw either saying 'Try again' or awarding a prize).
- **Golden egg.** Collect as many empty egg shells as you can and put them in a tray of sand. Place a coin or small prize under some of them and wrapped sweets under the others. Contestants pay to pick up a shell and win whatever is underneath.
- **Wash day challenge.** String up a washing line with plenty of wooden or plastic pegs on it. Challenge people to see how many pegs they can remove and hold with one hand before dropping them. Keep score and award a prize to the man, woman and child with the highest score at the end of the event.

Sell programmes, which can double as entry tickets, in advance of the fair and at the gate. Invite local businesses to take advertising space and use it to thank your supporters and sponsors. Have a wonderful time!

***

See also: How do I make it safe and legal?; Alcohol (liquor) licensing; Food safety; Licensing – playing live and recorded music and Lotteries and non-commercial gaming and betting.

5
Out and about

Scarecrow trail

A scarecrow trail is a fun event which will bring a community together and raise awareness of your charity or cause. They are generally held on a weekend or a week during a school holiday.

Volunteers sign up to build a scarecrow to sit, stand or even recline in front of their home or business. Scarecrow hunters buy a map showing where the scarecrows are and are encouraged to complete a puzzle which can only be solved by using clues on or by the different scarecrows. Correct and returned entry forms are placed in a draw and the winner(s) awarded a prize.

The scarecrows could be dressed as characters from fairy tales or nursery rhymes, famous people or comic characters, depending on your theme. Why not hold a scarecrow making day when people can get to know each other and share ideas as they stick, sew, paint and stuff?

Invite the local media to take photographs, and use the scarecrow images on your posters and flyers, website and social media. You may even be able to persuade some of your volunteers to dress up as scarecrows to deliver leaflets publicising the event.

Ask local shop owners if they would let you put a scarecrow in their window, or better still display one of their own, with information about the event. Stand them in gardens on main routes to local schools, churches and shops.

Appoint a scarecrow judge – perhaps the art teacher at a local school – to award a prize for the best scarecrow or ask the scarecrow hunters to vote for their favourite.

Sell advertising space on the map and encourage local shops and pubs to sell them to their customers. Set up a scarecrow headquarters along the trail where you can sell maps, serve refreshments and provide other scarecrow-themed fundraising attractions. Stick lollies into a giant corn cob made from polystyrene for a lucky lolly game. Sell scarecrow pictures for youngsters to colour. Hold a children's scarecrow fancy dress competition. Transform cupcakes and biscuits into scarecrows and birds and serve scarecrow pie (cottage pie), scarecrow jackets (stuffed jacket potatoes) and wiggly worms (pasta and sauce). Sell popcorn, foil-wrapped chocolate 'bugs' and gum or jelly 'worms'.

Treasure hunt

There are various kinds of treasure hunts. They may not make vast profits but there are few overheads and they're good fun. If possible choose a weekend or a summer evening when it's light and people will be keen to get out of doors. A basic hunt is usually on foot around a local area or community. This is likely to attract whole families, so it needs to be fairly simple and over a safe and easy route. Find someone who knows the area well and is good at organising to set the hunt and prepare the clues. Charge a small fee per individual, couple or family to take part. Set a finish time and fix up a rendezvous where treasure hunters can head if they get lost or give up. Announce the winners at the rendezvous and award a small prize or prizes.

If you know anyone with a large garden, an alternative might be to sprinkle the clues in and around the greenhouse, potting shed and flowers.

For the more adventurous, there's the car treasure hunt where teams pay a fee per vehicle to enter. This is far more challenging as it's over a longer route and the clues are more difficult to find if people don't know the area. It would be prudent to liaise with the local police, who will be able to advise on black spots to avoid.

If more than 12 vehicles are taking part the event will need to be authorised by the Royal Automobile Club Motor Sports Association Competition Authorisation Office (England and Wales) or the Royal Scottish Automobile Club (Scotland). Visit the Motor Sports Association website (www.msauk.org) for advice on running a successful car trea-sure hunt.

Whether you're hunting for treasure on foot or by car, appoint one or two people who have not been involved with setting the clues to do a dry run a few days before the event to check the clues make sense and that nothing you're relying on has been moved or changed.

Give your competitors a sealed envelope with details of how to find the rendezvous in case they get lost.

Open gardens

Are there keen gardeners in your community who would be willing to share their passion for plants by opening their gardens to the public to help your cause?

Admiring other people's gardens and gaining hints and tips to transform your own – as well as seeing how other people live – has been a British pastime for hundreds of years. It started with the tradition of the wealthy and aristocratic opening their gates to the interested and curious. Remember Elizabeth Bennet stopping off to nose around Mr Darcy's home and garden in *Pride and Prejudice*?

The gardens don't need to be big. They could be low maintenance, wildlife havens or famed for their display of hanging baskets, container pots or even garden gnomes. Try and encourage at least five homes to take part. Encourage your visitors to come on foot but think about where people should park and which gardens are accessible for wheelchair users. Gardeners will want to mow the lawn and get everything shipshape, but it's also important they make sure paths and steps are safe. Ask your gardeners to check that their visitors are covered under their home insurance and have umbrellas at the gate and extra loo rolls in store!

Choose a Sunday or bank holiday when your gardeners will be at home and people are more likely to be looking for something to do. Provide a programme with details of all of the gardens and a map of how to find them, indicating where refreshments will be served. Ask local garden centres, garden equipment suppliers, tree surgeons and landscaping and garden maintenance companies to buy advertising space in the programme.

Charge visitors for the programme, which would also serve as the entry ticket to the gardens. The more gardens which are open, the more you can charge. Sell as many programmes as you can in advance. This will give you a good idea as to how many cakes and cups, chairs and tables you will need to set up at your refreshment stops. Sitting around and eating cake and drinking freshly brewed tea or coffee is as much a part of an open garden event as the gardens themselves. Serve cream teas, coffee and homemade cakes and biscuits in the largest and most suitable gardens. Think about what to do if it rains – is there a conservatory or pop-up gazebo where guests can drink their tea in the dry?

If it's just not practical to serve refreshments in one or more of your gardens, book the local church or community hall.

Recruit volunteers to bake, help bring in extra tables and chairs, make the hot drinks, serve the visitors and clear up afterwards. Sell plants or other garden produce in one of the gardens or at your refreshment stop.

Advertise the event in local garden centres and shops and distribute posters and flyers. Tell the local media what you're doing and why.

If you want to attract visitors from a wider area think about listing your open day on the Open Gardens website (www.opengardens.co.uk), which advertises town and village open garden events for charity free of charge.

Raft race

Building rafts from plastic drums and timber offcuts and then putting them through their paces is still popular in today's age of computer games. Raft races aren't the easiest of fundraisers to organise but they can raise substantial amounts of money and are great fun for the rafters and spectators alike.

First you need to find a suitable stretch of water with easy and safe access points to launch the rafts and then return them to dry land at the end of the race. You'll need to get the permission of the owner of any river, lake or water park and any adjacent land you need to use. In the case of public land, this will be the local authority. Contact your local water or river authority to identify private owners.

Risks posed by running water provide an additional challenge. Make sure you have adequate insurance to protect yourself, or the organisation or charity you are supporting, from any claims if any property is damaged or anyone is injured. Some insurers exclude hazardous activities such as raft races, so you may need to take out specific insurance cover for your event. Do a thorough risk assessment and take any safety measures which may be required. This might include appointing safety crews and first aiders, erecting barriers, roping off areas that are slippery or hazardous, appointing marshals to ensure that spectators, particularly children, don't get too close to the water and issuing water safety guidance, etc. The owner or owners of the water may also want to impose their own conditions.

Fix a date – bearing in mind you will need plenty of time to organise the event and your rafters will need time to build their vessels.

Draw up rules about permitted and banned construction materials and equipment (for example water cannon), the method of construction and the overall size of the rafts. Stipulate that rafts should be light enough for the rafters to carry in and out of the water. Do you want to allow pedal-powered rafts or paddles only? Are there any low bridges which would limit the height of masts? Set rules too for the rafters – for instance a maximum number per raft and that life jackets must be worn. Appoint a scrutineer to ban any rafts which break the rules or are considered to be unsafe from entering the water.

Speak to your local authority or the Health and Safety Executive if you need any assistance.

Garages, hotels, businesses, factories – particularly those with apprentices – sports clubs and Student Unions are prime places to 'press gang' your rafters.

Work closely with your local media – they may even want to take part!

Set a theme and award prizes for the best constructed raft, the best dressed raft and crew, the race winners and the team who raised the most sponsorship.

Try to find a sponsor or sponsors to cover your fixed costs such as insurance, safety crews, barriers, first aid facilities and prizes. Charge an entry fee for each craft and ask each crew to raise sponsorship money.

Put the rafts 'on parade' before the race to encourage last-minute sponsorship, and make the most of the crowd at the finish by providing other fundraising activities to keep spectators entertained – and spending.

Go-kart derby

Homemade go-karts built out of old pram or bike wheels, a central plank and a seat for the driver, used to be a familiar sight in parks and cul-de-sacs. Increases in traffic and concerns about safety have taken their toll, but go-kart derbies remain a worthwhile event in the fundraiser's repertoire.

Find a suitable 'race track' – look for a field, sports ground or empty car park – and set rules for the construction of the karts, the drivers and pushers and their conduct on the race track. If you want to use a local road, contact your local authority for advice and guidance on what arrangements would need to be made to close the road.

It's important to get enough entrants to run at least one race. If you're confident there are plenty of closet racers in your community, you may want to hold races for different age groups, men, women, etc. Advertise for entries and invite local groups, sports clubs and businesses as well as individuals to enter karts. Don't forget to include older people – they may have plenty of experience of go-kart building and racing from their childhood that they can pass on.

Instead of racing you could set a time challenge with competitors completing a set distance or course against the clock.

The more unconventional and eye-catching the kart, the better. Award prizes for the most innovative kart, best constructed kart, etc, as well as first past the post or fastest against the clock. Charge an entry fee and ask every team to raise sponsorship money for your cause. As with similar events, try and cover your overheads by finding an overall sponsor or sponsors for the derby and for each race.

Go-kart derbies, and similar activities which insurers view as hazardous, may be excluded under your organisation or charity's public liability insurance. If this is the case, or you are running the event independently, you will need to take out separate insurance for your event. This will need to include employer's liability for your volunteers.

Do a full risk assessment and recruit marshals, first aiders, etc. Appoint a scrutineer to check the safety of each go-kart before the race. Encourage the media to publicise the race and offer them photos and photo opportunities. Use posters and banners to draw people to the derby.

Your go-kart derby could be a stand-alone event or a main attraction at a sports club or community fair.

***

See also: How do I make it safe and legal?; Food safety and Sponsorship.

6

Sponsorship and sport

Sponsorship

Personal challenges are a great way to raise money for a charity or cause that's dear to your heart. You can get sponsorship for almost anything, from giving up your guilty pleasures to running a marathon or jumping out of an aeroplane at 13,000ft. Hair shaving or hair raising – the choice is yours!

The key to success is getting sponsors. The more, the better. This is not a time to be a shrinking violet – if you don't ask, you won't get! Tell everyone you know what you will be doing and ask them to sponsor you. Start with your family, your friends, your colleagues at work and your neighbours.

If you are fundraising for a registered charity or cause, such as an amateur sports club, they will be able to claim Gift Aid from the government on individual donations, provided the sponsor is a UK taxpayer and has paid sufficient tax. Ask your charity or cause for sponsorship forms.

Set up your own online donation page on a site such as www.justgiving.com or www.virginmoneygiving.com. They will take a small percentage towards the cost of running the service but offer a secure way for people to donate to you online and enable your sponsors to pay by credit or debit card. This will also make it easier for family and friends who do not live locally to support you. Share your page on social media and email a link to friends and contacts.

Approach people who you think are likely to pledge the most first – your family or even your boss. If the first few pledges on the form are generous, there's a good chance that the sponsors who follow them will be generous too. Some fundraisers like to set themselves a personal challenge to raise £100, £1,000 or more. If so, tell everyone how much you're hoping to raise – you might even persuade your employer or other sponsor to match the money you raise. Let your sponsors know when you plan to collect their pledges. If they offer to pay when they sign up, take their pledges there and then!

If something happens and you are unable to take part, or the event is cancelled, contact all your donors and ask if they are still happy for the money they have pledged to go to your good cause. If not, any money paid in advance must be refunded.

If your charity or good cause is not well known, be prepared to explain why it's important to you and see if you can obtain flyers and leaflets to hand out. Is there a noticeboard at work where you can post details of your event or a staff newsletter or intranet which would give you publicity?

The more attention you can generate, the more successful your fund-raising will be. The more unusual, imaginative or out of character your challenge, the better. Contact your local media and tell them what you're doing and why. If you are raising money for something that has affected you or a member of your family, share your story. Is there a photo opportunity you can think of which would draw people's eyes to your story and help drive potential sponsors to your sponsorship page?

Keep your sponsors up to date with your progress and ask someone to film and take pictures on the day. Share them with your sponsors on Facebook and YouTube. Chase up any outstanding pledges and thank everyone who supported you.

Want to be sponsored but can't think what to do?

Dress down (or up) day

Organise a day at work, college or school when everyone is dressed in casual clothing, fancy dress, or dressed from head to toe in one colour. Ask colleagues taking part to donate £1 and ask those who don't to pay a 'fine'.

Sponsored silence

Do you talk too much? How about promising to take a vow of silence and ask people to pay up for you to shut up?

Phone-free day or week

Always glued to your phone? Go cold turkey and have a phone-free day or week.

Sponsored slim

Is it time your friends saw rather less of you? How about a sponsored diet?

Give up a guilty pleasure

Get sponsored to stop smoking, drinking alcohol, eating chocolate, watching TV soaps, or any other guilty pleasure.

Baked bean bath

How about taking a baked bean bath? People will always pay to see you do something embarrassing or uncomfortable! Top up your sponsorship money by inviting onlookers to pay to help fill up your bath with baked beans – which they're likely to pour over your head! Choose a venue where plenty of people can enjoy the spectacle!

Head shave or hair dye

If you're looking for something a bit more dramatic how about a head shave or hair dye? If you want to go wackier, think about being sponsored to sport a half-shaved head, half a moustache or a half-dyed head of hair. You'll turn heads and people will ask you about your new look, giving you the ideal opportunity to tell them about the charity or good cause you're fundraising for. Hold the event in a venue where your supporters can watch and cheer you on!

Dog walk or dog carry

You'd rather be out and about? Perhaps a sponsored dog walk, or better still a dog carry, especially if your pet's a Great Dane!

Cycle ride, tandem bike ride, litter pick

How about a sponsored cycle ride, tandem bike ride or litter pick?

Parachute jump, skydive, abseil, bungee jump or fire walk

Need something a little more extreme?

- **Parachute jump.** Is stepping out of an aeroplane several thousand feet above the ground scary enough? If you're a novice jumper, expect to do a static cord jump. A cord is attached to the aeroplane at one end and the bag in which your parachute is packed at the other. As you fall from the aircraft the line deploys the parachute. An instructor then uses a radio attached to your helmet to guide you down to the landing area.
- **Tandem skydive.** In skydiving the jumper leaves the plane and goes into freefall for a short time before the parachute is deployed. As you'll be firmly attached to an experienced instructor it's ideal for novices and older or less able people.
- **Charity abseil.** Abseiling involves sliding down a rope from a bridge, viaduct, tall building or other landmark. Buildings with flat roofs such as hospitals, university accommodation and fire station towers all make great venues – provided you've got permission to use them!
- **Bungee jump.** Bungee jumping involves plunging from a high bridge or a crane while attached to a large elastic cord. One end of the rope is attached to the top of the bridge or crane cage and the other to an ankle harness and back-up waist harness. The cord breaks your fall and leaves you bouncing around before you're either lowered to the ground or hauled back up to the top of the bridge or other platform.

- **Fire or ice walk.** Want to keep your feet on the ground? Are you brave enough to walk barefoot over hot coals or broken glass? A path of burning coal is laid within a track cut into the turf of a sports ground or field. The coals are lit well in advance of the fire walk and have to be at just the right temperature before it is safe to attempt the walk. The event is held at night so the glowing coals are visible through the layer of ash covering them. Glass walking, which is also known as ice walking, involves walking over glass from hundreds of broken and sterilised bottles.

Above all, it's important that your fundraising is not only fun but safe. Running these sorts of challenges is a job for the experts. An online search will bring up a number of options. The best companies and clubs have years of experience and can advise you on where to hold your event as well as providing training, specialist equipment and insurance. What they offer varies – so shop around. Many companies will also be able to provide advice on getting sponsorship and give you a photograph or video of your 'derring do' which you can share with friends and relatives on Facebook and YouTube.

If you don't think you'll be able to get enough like-minded people together to have your own event, many companies offer spaces at corporate events where everyone raises money for their own good cause. Some charities run their own events and will pay for your place provided you commit to raising a minimum amount. If you're taking the costs of your challenge out of sponsorship money, you must make this clear to your donors. As you will have received a benefit (because you did not pay the full costs yourself), Gift Aid may not be available on donations by anyone connected to you – for instance a partner, parent or child. Visit the Gift Aid rules (see Useful contacts and resources) for information.

Do your sums. It could cost hundreds of pounds to take part in a parachute jump or skydive. Unless you're willing to pay those costs yourself, you'll need to find enough sponsors to cover the cost of your place before you can make any money for your cause or charity.

Marathons

Marathons are a well-established way of raising money for good causes. But they're not for the unfit or the faint-hearted!

The run itself is 26.2 footslogging miles (42.2 kilometres) and requires a punishing training regime before the event.

You'll find plenty of advice on how to train on running club and charity websites. You could even make new friends, as well as helping your cause, by joining a local running club and training with others.

Competition to take part in one of the large events, such as the London marathon, is fierce and you'll need to register as early as possible. Most events reserve a set number of places for specific charities, so if you're running for a major charity, apply for one of their places.

If a full marathon isn't for you, there are plenty of alternatives – half marathons (13.1 miles, 21.1 kilometres) such as Bristol, Birmingham, Cardiff and the Great Scottish Run – as well as a wealth of shorter fun runs throughout the UK.

You can increase your donations, your chances of gaining media coverage and your spectators' enjoyment by wearing fancy dress. If you are raising money for your local baby unit don a frilly bonnet and bib together with a giant nappy and dummy. Raising money to help disadvantaged people at Christmas? How about dressing as a Christmas pudding or turkey?

Fun run

If you're raising money for a local charity why not organise your own fun run? Search your local authority website for advice and information on holding events on the highway and in public places. Encourage your runners to wear fancy dress by awarding prizes for the best costumes. Get as much publicity as you can. Your runners will get a real boost when they see people looking out of windows and lining the streets to cheer them on.

Marathon-style events

If running's not your forte, there are plenty of other marathon-style events to consider such as a dance-a-thon (dancing constantly for a set period of time), swim-a-thon or other activity.

You could even cycle from Land's End to John O'Groats or row or swim the English Channel without leaving your local sports centre. Calculate how long it would take to do the distance on an exercise bike, on a rowing machine or in the pool. If it's too far for you, or the time available is limited, recruit a team with each member doing a set distance, either in relay or concurrently. You'll raise more money that way too, as each team member will be seeking sponsors. Why not get permission to take your exercise bikes or rowing machines to a local shopping centre so that your supporters can collect donations from passing shoppers?

(If the open road's for you, note that if you're planning to seek donations en route, you'll need a street collection licence from each licensing authority you pass through.)

Keep an eye on the news for ideas. Is there a group of intrepid explorers about to set off to the Antarctic? Pay your own tribute by dragging a laden sleigh for a set time or over a fixed distance around a playing field or other venue. Get your supporters to dress as penguins and abominable snowmen and encourage spectators to watch and cheer you on, fortified by bacon butties and mugs of tea or coffee.

Sponsored jailbreak

Break out of jail with the help of your local police, or, if you live near an ancient lock-up, the museum curator, and see how far you can travel for free in 12 or 24 hours. Ask friends and colleagues to sponsor you for every mile you travel.

Travel in small teams for safety reasons – and restrict entry to adults only. Dress the part to encourage people to help you on your way. Paint crow's feet on a pair of all-in-one overalls and attach a plastic chain or rope to an old ball to create your very own ball and chain. If you're aiming to leave the UK, make sure you have a passport, travel insurance and a debit or credit card that works abroad. Take a map of the UK and some 'Hitching for charity' banners if you're looking for lifts. Be clear how much of your own money you're prepared to commit. Bear in mind that you may have escaped to the south of France – but you've still got to get back!

Golf day

If golf's your sport then why not tee off a charity golf day? Invite teams of four (or two) to enter. Add to the fun with a twos competition, a challenge to see who can make the straightest drive, or a contest to find the player who can land a tee shot nearest the pin. Arrange for tea and coffee on arrival and ask your clubhouse caterers if they'll provide a sit-down meal or buffet. Tell them you're raising money for charity and ask if they will give you a reduced rate.

Publicise the event on the internet, at other golf clubs, in sports shops and through the media. Award prizes for the best ladies', men's and mixed teams as well as your individual fun events. Make your money by charging an entrance fee and extra to take part in any team or individual challenges.

Sports tournament

What better way to kick start your fundraising than a sports tournament? Arrange a friendly football, rounders, netball, hockey or other team sport tournament. Charge an entry fee and award a cup to the winning team with small prizes – such as promotional items – to the winning players. Add some fun prizes along the way for the best dressed player,  muddiest player, niftiest footwork, best mover, etc.

Encourage players' friends and relatives to attend by serving hot drinks and light refreshments. Do you have supporters who could run a cake or plant stall, sell second-hand sports equipment or run other fundraising activities?

It's a knockout

Inflatable obstacle courses, bizarre costumes and mad games – tumbling around in a giant foam-filled washing machine or building a giant burger – it's a knockout fundraiser!

There's even a company that says it owns and uses the original props and games from the BBC TV *It's a Knockout* show.

Expect to pay from around £4,200 plus VAT for an event for 100 competitors, to include an array of games, the wacky costumes, PA system, compère and knockout crew plus trophies and medals for the winners.

Cover the cost of the event by seeking an overall sponsor, or sponsors, for the tournament and for individual games and charge an entry fee for each team.

Add as many extra attractions and fundraisers as you can accommodate and staff.

Silly sports day

Don't leave all the sports day fun to the youngsters. How about running an all-age silly sports day with races for everyone from the very young to the not so young? Think of the old favourites, and add some of your own.

- **Egg and spoon, potato and spoon or even football and spoon race.**
- **Pancake race.**
- **Chef and waiter race.**
- **Three-legged race.** Make one a parent and child race – not as easy as you might think!

- **Sack race.**
- **100m sprint.** Even better if the runners are in fancy dress, with a prize for the best costume.
- **Wheelbarrow race.**
- **Leap frog.**
- **Under frog.** Contestants crawl through an obstacle course of tables or chairs.
- **Tug of war.**
- **Late for work relay.** Line your teams up, half at one end of the 'track' and half at the other. The first person in each team runs to a pile of adult-size clothes in the middle of the track (hat, sunglasses, tie or scarf, wellies or shoes, jacket, coat or heavy sweater), puts them all on and then runs to their team mates at the other end, where they undress and pass the clothes to the next runner.
- **Spider race.** Contestants race on their hands and feet with their bottoms in the air as if they are spiders.
- **Matchbox race.** Teams stand in line with their hands behind their backs. First player has to pick up a matchbox sleeve with their nose and then pass it on to the nose of the next player.
- **Space hopper race.** Buy your hoppers second-hand on eBay and ask supporters to check whether they've any lurking in their garage or loft. At the end of the race sell or auction any you don't want to keep.

Raise funds by charging competitors a small entry fee for each race, selling refreshments and adding other 'sports' such as a coconut shy or welly wanging (see Fairs and fun days).

Pub sports day

Ask a local pub to sponsor a day of sporting activities to help your charity or cause (and their bar takings!). Offer to provide volunteers to help run a pub sport olympics event with team and individual games such as darts, table tennis, pool, billiards or bar billiards, dominoes, shove ha'penny, pitch penny and skittles. Negotiate a commission for your charity on bar and food sales and charge players a fee to take part in each game. Round the day off with a sporting quiz and don't forget a raffle, beer glass tombola (see Lotteries and non-commercial gaming and betting), silent auction or other fundraiser.

World record attempt

The world's tallest plastic brick tower, the fastest time to eat a muffin (with no hands), the most sticky notes to be stuck on a face in one minute. The weird, the wonderful and the plain extraordinary – it's all in the Guinness World Records. Borrow a copy of the annual book from your local library, go online, or invest in a personal copy to find records to challenge or wacky ideas for fun contests at fairs and fun days.

***

See also: How do I make it safe and legal?; Food safety and Street and door-to-door collections.

7
Auctions, sales and services

Auction

Going, going, gone! Auctioning goods and services for charity is a time-honoured way to raise funds, either as an event in itself or as part of a charity dinner or other activity.

First you need something to go 'under the hammer'. This can be new or second-hand items or skills and services donated by members and supporters of your organisation. Next you need an auctioneer with the gift of the gab – to encourage friendly rivalry – and excellent time management.

Auctions need two bursts of activity – the first to get items to auction, the second to attract as many people as possible to attend and bid. Approach everyone you know, and any companies you think might wish to support you, or use your auction to promote their services, to see if they are able to offer suitable items or services. The most sought after lots at auctions are often ones that money can't buy, for instance a tour of the local TV or radio station, lunch with a VIP, signed football shirts or a ride in a vintage car. Do you know anyone who might be able to help you secure this kind of lot?

Prepare a list of your lots to encourage bidders and help the auctioneer to determine how best to conduct the sale in the time available. In a traditional auction the auctioneer will set a price to start the bidding and then encourage increasingly higher bids from the audience until a bid price is reached above which no-one is willing to pay more. The person who made the final, highest bid then owns the item on payment of that sum.

If you're in the enviable position of having too many items to get through, you may want to think about holding a silent auction for some of your items and announcing the results at a set time during your event. It's disheartening to see people leaving with money they'd intended to spend in their pockets because the auction has overrun, the items they were interested in buying are still way down the auctioneer's list, and the babysitter's time is up.

Mini auctions are a good way of adding to the profits from another event, for instance auctioning off any fruit and vegetables donated during a harvest festival or the prize-winning cake at a cake competition. It's also worth considering a Dutch auction. A Dutch auction is the opposite of the traditional auction. It's less widely used but is useful if you need to auction goods quickly, as only one bid is needed to secure a sale. The auctioneer begins with a high asking price which is progressively lowered until someone indicates they'll buy.

If you're worried that items could be sold too cheaply, you can always set a reserve price. Items which didn't sell could then be offered at the reserve price.

Auction of promises

Nearly everyone supporting your charity or cause will have something they can do that people will pay money to experience, or to avoid having to do the job themselves!

Auctions of promises work best when the bidders and the people who are offering the services are known to each other and bidders are better able to judge the level of expertise on offer. Profitable promises include:

- car washing
- ironing
- gardening
- cooking a meal
- babysitting
- computer help
- painting and decorating
- cleaning
- beauty treatments
- use of a holiday home
- maths, guitar or singing tuition, etc
- a homemade cake.

Silent auction

A silent auction is an ideal partner for a dinner or award ceremony but could also be used at fairs and other events or alongside a traditional auction.

A list of items is displayed or circulated at the beginning of the event. Bidders are each given envelopes and sheets of paper on which they write their name, the number of the lot they are interested in, and how much they are prepared to bid to secure it. Each bid is placed in an envelope and then handed to the organiser. The bids are opened and the highest bidder for each item wins it.

Another method is to attach a list to each of the items and invite bidders to write their name and bid on the list attached to the item they're interested in bidding for, giving their contact details to the organiser. Anyone else who is interested would then add their name and higher bid to the list. The most sought-after items will attract many bids with bidders returning to the list during the event to see if their bid is still the highest and, if not, to decide whether to increase it. The winning bids are then announced at the end of the event.

Online auctions

eBay has turned auctioning donated and unloved items into an every-day activity for millions of people. Groups or individuals can help their chosen cause by donating anything between 10–100% of the final sell-ing price through the eBay for Charity programme.

eBay also reduces the insertion and final value fees on charity items equivalent to the percentage you donate. So if you donate 50% of the selling price to charity, eBay will waive 50% of your fees. Items which are being sold for charity are flagged with a blue and yellow ribbon, along with the percentage of any donation. Buyers are often willing to pay more if they know their money is going to charity.

If you are an individual UK taxpayer, Pay Pal will reclaim Gift Aid on the percentage you have donated, boosting your donation by 25p for every £1 you give. The money raised is paid direct to your nominated cause or charity. If your cause or charity is not already registered on the site, simply visit www.ebay.co.uk and sign up.

Registered charities can also sign up to sell their own items on eBay and collect 100% of the final sale price.

You may be able to run an online auction on your company or organisation's website or through your employer's intranet. List the goods or services you want to sell – and explain the difference that the money raised will make to people's lives. Anyone viewing the site can make a bid until a final deadline when the highest bid wins. This idea works particularly well with auctions of promises in the workplace.

Charity wristbands, badges and pins

Charity wristbands, badges, tie or lapel pins, sticky bugs, fridge magnets, pens and other promotional items can be bought for a few pence each and are a well-established way to raise awareness of a charity or cause. Wherever possible, include your charity or good cause's internet address on the item to encourage people to visit their website.

Depending on your objectives, charge a set price, give them away, or use them as prizes.

The more creative or striking your item, the more likely it is that friends, and even strangers, will ask you about it, giving you the opportunity to tell people about your cause.

Plenty of companies offer this sort of promotional merchandise and it's possible to place a minimum order for just 50, making it suitable for both large and small organisations. The more you order, the lower the price you pay per item.

Plastic or metal pin badges – think of the badges with ages or cheeky quips which are attached to birthday cards – can be produced for you, or you can make your own by buying or hiring a badge machine.

Sell your promotional items at your events. Use them to say 'thank you' to your helpers – particularly children – and as prizes at fundraising events.

Create your own merchandise

Creating and selling your own items – such as Christmas cards, cal-endars, coasters, mugs, T-shirts and tea towels – is a tried and tested way of raising the profile of your charity or good cause and bringing in the cash. These schemes work best where there are a large number of prospective purchasers – for instance a school, sports club or church congregation. There are plenty of people offering to create custom-ised merchandise – search online to get the best possible deal.

The organisation generally supplies its own image, which could be a drawing, good quality photograph or some text, to a company which specialises in creating this type of merchandise. The organisation then sells the items and retains the profit. You can reduce any risk of being left with dozens of unsold items, as well as calculating your profits in advance, by asking people to pay a deposit or the full price of the item before you place your order.

If you think your items might appeal to a wider group of people, you may want to order extra to sell at your events and on eBay. Approach local traders to see if they would be willing to sell them on your behalf.

Buy a brick

Looking to fund a new building or an extension? Buy-a-brick schemes are a great way to raise the profile of your project and capture peo-ple's imagination, giving your supporters a feeling of ownership and involvement. They're also eligible for Gift Aid.

Ask people to sponsor a brick or tile for a fixed donation – which will be more than the actual cost of the brick. Involve anyone with any connection with your building or cause, for instance past and pres-ent members of your club or current and former members of your congregation. Ask the sponsor to write their name on the back of the brick or tile in permanent marker pen, or offer to do it on their behalf.

Get permission from local supermarkets, shopping centres and offices to sell bricks in their car park or complex. Ask the builders or company supplying the bricks if they can help you with the logistics – it's good publicity for them too.

Don't want to be a 'brickie'? There are plenty of alternative ways to run buy-a-brick schemes ranging from asking donors to add their names to buy-a-brick posters to sponsoring a virtual 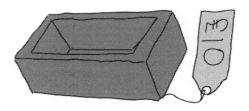 brick in a website 'wall'. The buyer gives their name and their message, which could relate to a special occasion or commemorate a loved one, and is given a certificate with the number of the brick they have sponsored. The message is revealed every time someone clicks on 'their' brick.

Sell the bricks online, at your fundraising events and piggyback on other people's events in your area by asking if you can have, or hire, a suitable space.

Write a book

You may feel there are easier ways of making money – and indeed there are! But you don't need to write a novel or encyclopaedia. Could you write a short story for children – perhaps based in your local town or community – or edit a collection of poems provided by members of your congregation, club or school? How about compiling a booklet of local walks with interesting things to look out for or writing a local history?

Keep an eye out for similar books to the one you have in mind. Look inside to see who published them and search on the internet for the best publishing options. Many of the booklets and guides you see available at the back of churches, at fairs or in the local Post Office are self-published, where the author bears the cost of publication of their book in the hope of recouping their outlay – and more. Some publishing companies will not only assist you with getting your book into print or digital format, but can also advise you on how to market it. If your book features your local pub, ask the licensee if they would be willing to have copies on sale in the bar. Local toy and book shops might be willing to sell your children's story book.

Give your book a plug on your organisation or charity's website. Offer copies for sale through your website (don't forget to add postage and packaging costs). Send a copy to your local paper or radio station and offer yourself for interview. See if your local bookshop would be willing to arrange a book signing event for you. Keep an eye out for events where you could have a small stand to tell people about your book and the charity or cause you're supporting and, of course, sell your book.

Invest time in researching your market – you don't want to end up with dozens of books you can't sell.

Compile a recipe book

Recipe books make an excellent Christmas stocking filler, birthday present or 'thank you' gift.

Ask everyone to contribute their favourite recipe. If it's one that's been in the family for generations and there's a story behind it, include that in the book as well. If possible, include recipes from people who will be known to those you hope will purchase your book. For instance, if you're raising money for a school, ask the head teacher if they would be willing to contribute.

Group your recipes into starters, main meals, cakes and biscuits, etc and shop around for a printer to turn them into a book. Most good printers will be able to offer you a design service and help you select bindings and covers. There are also a number of websites which provide templates so you can do the whole process online. Boost your profits by asking local businesses and traders if they'd like to advertise in the book – and see if they'd be willing to help sell copies at their reception desks or shops.

It's important to respect other people's copyright, so you need to tread with some care to avoid passing off Nigella's culinary creation as your own. Obviously there are umpteen recipes around for Eton mess, tomato and basil soup or sponge cake – the ingredients are likely to be the same and some will have exactly the same proportions of ingredients. If a published recipe has been changed slightly, for instance by using blueberries instead of strawberries, it's considered ethical to use 'based on' or 'adapted from' to credit the source of the recipe. It's also important to re-write the recipe in your own words. If in doubt, approach the author of the recipe or the publishing house of the magazine or book in which the recipe appeared. Sharing recipes is an age-old tradition and the writer may even be willing to support your charity and raise the profile of your book by donating a recipe of their own.

Product parties

Some readers may well recall attending a Tupperware party – where friends and neighbours would gather in the hostess's home to see a demonstration of Earl Tupper's brightly coloured food containers with their 'burping' airtight seal. The party hostess would earn commission on anything purchased at her party and a bonus if any of her guests booked their own party.

Product parties – including Tupperware – are still going strong and these days you can boost your funds by marketing anything from underwear and cosmetics to greetings cards and kitchen equipment.

Find a product that you like and you think your friends and neighbours might also like. Invite as many people as you can comfortably squeeze into your home, or if that's not as many as you'd like, think about holding a bigger event in a school or church hall. Ask the party plan consultant to pay the commission in cash rather than goods. Make sure your guests have a good time by making the product presentation part of the show, and not the whole show. If you think your guests would like a make-up party, ask the sales agent if she will do a makeover for some or all of your guests. If kitchen equipment is more your line, why not build in a mini cooking demonstration using the products and invite guests to sample the freshly cooked food? Encourage your guests to get to know each other. Offer light refreshments and consider adding a small raffle or other fundraising activity.

Raise funds over a longer period by circulating catalogues and flyers for the product, collecting orders and delivering products.

Make and sell your own items

Love knitting or crochet? The most important thing is to think carefully about what to make and who might want to buy those items. Keep up to date with modern trends and styles. Are fingerless gloves and knitted cushion covers 'in' or out? What colours or patterns are in vogue? Children's hats, gloves and mittens are usually reliable sellers. Special outfits for dolls and teddy bears are also likely to find a loving home. Novelty knitted items such as quirky tea cosies, and Christmas and Easter decorations are also likely to sell well. Look online and in libraries and magazines for patterns and fresh ideas. Why not take orders for larger, bespoke items such as jumpers or knitted jackets and donate your fee to your chosen charity?

If your talent lies in needlework, greetings cards, jewellery, basket weaving, candle making, woodwork, pottery, stained glass or other craft, look for fairs and other events to market your items or sell them through eBay and donate some or all of the sale price.

Balloon models

These are always a hit with children. Go online to source special balloons for modelling or see what's available at your local party shop. You could hire a balloon artist to produce animals and other shapes to order or hold a balloon modelling workshop where people can have a go at making their own designs. Charge an entry fee or fee per model to cover your costs and make a profit.

Craft fair

It's no surprise that the majority of craft fairs are held in November or December, when people relish the opportunity to hunt for that perfect gift, stocking filler or decoration. There's lots of useful advice on running craft fairs to be found on the internet and there may well be people in your community with experience of running them who would be happy to share their knowledge and experience.

The first thing to do is to decide when and where you want to run your fair, and for how long. Most community craft fairs are held at weekends and run from around 10am to 4pm. Church, community and school halls make ideal venues as they're likely to have toilets, good accessibility, plenty of tables and chairs and catering facilities.

Try to source a wide range of craftspeople. Search the internet and local residents' guides and community websites for ideas and contacts. Visit other craft fairs to identify exhibitors whose work might prove attractive to the people who are likely to attend your fair, and ask for their contact details.

Charge the exhibitors enough to cover the cost of the venue, promotional material and any other expenses. In return, they will expect you to do your best to attract as many visitors as possible on the day to ensure they have sufficient opportunity to recoup their fee and make a profit.

Draw up a plan detailing where each stall will be located, making sure that similar crafts aren't placed next to each other. Keep in touch with your exhibitors so they're clear when, where, and what time the fair is open, when you expect them to arrive to set up, who they need to report to when they arrive, any responsibilities, such as clearing up, and how you plan to publicise the event.

Raise money by charging an entrance fee, selling your own merchandise and refreshments and adding a raffle, silent auction or other fundraising activities.

Plant sale

A plant sale can be an event in itself, or part of a bigger fundraiser such as an open garden event, scarecrow trail, car boot sale, craft sale or community fair. They're easy to organise but need to be planned well in advance to allow everyone time to sow seeds, plant bulbs, take cuttings and pot plants so there's plenty to sell.

You'll also need to think about the timing. Late spring, summer or early autumn are all busy times for gardeners, who'll be on the lookout for new plants. Your sale can take place inside or out. Outdoors is always nicer, and will draw passing traffic, but have contingency plans in case of a deluge on the day.

Take along plenty of tables – picnic and wallpaper pasting tables are ideal – to display your wares and a supply of plastic bags and cardboard boxes so buyers can take the plants home without getting dirt on their clothes or car. You could group the plants by type – annuals, perennials, shrubs, bulbs, etc – or simply ask everyone to sell their contributions on their own stall.

Are any of your supporters famed for the magnificence of their hanging baskets? Get together before the event and make hanging baskets to sell. Plant bulbs in nice bowls or in cans with any sharp edges flattened and the sides decorated with wrapping paper and ribbon.

Offer homemade cake and hot drinks to encourage people to linger – passers-by will want to find out what's going on.

Car wash

Get out the sponges and wheel in the cash! All you need are sponges, car shampoo, buckets, chamois leathers to dry the cars, old towels or other clean rags, access to water and plenty of volunteers.

Research the cost of a car wash at local supermarkets or service stations and set your price accordingly. If you've got enough space to provide a dry area, a power supply, vacuum cleaners and sufficient volunteers, you may want to charge extra to clean and polish the interior.

Arrange your volunteers in shifts throughout the day with separate jobs.

- A 'salesman' to attract drivers and explain what they'll get for their money and why you're raising funds.
- A wash team to clean and rinse each car.
- A finishing team to get any water residue off.

Change the water frequently – ideally between each vehicle. Use new sponges and discard any sponges or rags which are dropped as they may have picked up dirt or grit which could scratch the cars.

Advertise your car wash by printing flyers and asking your local garages, car accessory shops, pubs and grocery stores to display them. Ask friends and neighbours to display them at work. Give contact details so motorists can book a slot and avoid having to hang around on the day. Post roadside signs on roads near the site a week or so ahead of the event and display a large board or banner at your venue to attract passing motorists (check what is permissible with your local authority).

If there's an opportunity to sell refreshments to customers while they wait for their car to be cleaned, take it.

Share your interest and expertise

Do you have a particular expertise or interest you can share with others? Offer to give family and friends a manicure or pedicure, walk your neighbours' dogs, mow their lawns, do their ironing, or offer your services as a babysitter and donate your earnings.

Doing something for others in return for a donation to your charity or cause not only raises funds but can boost self-esteem and give people a sense of being a part of their wider community.

Discover history on your doorstep. Organise a local walk or talk to share the history of where you live, highlighting how the area has changed over the centuries. Draw attention to historic buildings or places where famous people lived, and explain how local streets got their names.

Antiques your thing? How about holding your own antiques road-show? Invite people to bring their antiques – old toys, glassware, pottery, etc – for an informed opinion or possible valuation. Charge a fee for each item or ask guests to make a donation. Offer light refreshments to raise even more.

Face painting your forte? Offer your services at fairs, fun days and children's parties. (Make sure you have access to clean water. Only use paints which are water soluble and hypoallergenic, and ask parents to sign an indemnity form.)

Hold your own masterclass. If you're particularly good at something why not share your enthusiasm and experience by organising a small class and charging a fee to attend?

- Teaching knitting, embroidery, quilting, marquetry or wood carving is a great way to keep old crafts alive and put something back into the community.
- Offer a class in bicycle maintenance.
- Are you an ace in the kitchen? Could you teach others how to make pastry or bread, decorate cakes, or give a demonstration of vegetarian, Caribbean or Italian cookery?
- Run a jewellery making or flower arranging workshop (charge extra for materials).

- Share your love of gardening by showing others how to prune and take cuttings or make a hanging basket (charge extra for materials if you run a 'hands on' session).
- Love DIY? Could you show others how to tile, paint, hang wallpaper or do minor household repairs?
- Computers more your thing? How about helping others to develop their computer skills, learn how to upload and edit pictures, use email, shop online or buy and sell on eBay?
- Share your love of calligraphy, photography, bridge or anything else you enjoy and think others might too.

Pamper evening

There's nothing nicer than being pampered – unless it's being pampered to help a good cause.

Pamper evenings (or afternoons) are a great way for people to try out different treatments. Search your local directories and online to find professional therapists, beauticians, manicurists and make-up experts who might be willing to offer taster sessions or give a demonstration. Some might even be willing to give their services free or for a reduced rate in order to gain new customers. Bear in mind that Fridays and Saturdays are usually busy days for beauty therapists so if you're looking at a weekend event you'll need to book their services well in advance.

Some treatments, or clients, may require privacy, so make sure you have enough rooms or space to erect portable screens when you book your venue.

There are a variety of ways you can ensure everyone is properly pampered.

- Charge a small entrance fee, which could include light refreshments, and charge a set price for each treatment. Ask each therapist to bring a list with booking times on so guests can choose their slot on a first-come, first-served basis.
- Charge a higher ticket price to include a specific number of treatments. Customers book their treatments on a first-come, first-served basis.
- Ask guests to select and pay for their treatments in advance.

Check in advance that your therapists have the appropriate insurance for whatever treatment they are providing. Welcome them when they arrive and help them to feel at home. Give them drinks and something to eat so they feel pampered too! Provide your guests with a list of the therapists and their contact details so they can get in touch with them after the event.

Create a comfortable seating area where people can relax and chat while they're waiting for their treatments. Play relaxing music and offer hot and cold drinks. Boost your takings by holding a raffle or other activity.

New style – new look

Do all your clothes flatter your natural colouring and body shape or do you feel there's room for improvement? Do you have items in your wardrobe that 'don't look quite right' but you're not quite sure why? Perhaps it's time to hire an image consultant to help you, your supporters, and your cause.

An image consultant can advise on how to choose colours and clothing styles that will flatter and enhance your look and help you create the perfect wardrobe to suit your natural colouring, lifestyle and budget.

Colour Me Beautiful (www.colourmebeautiful.co.uk) and House of Colour (www.houseofcolour.co.uk) offer colour and style consultations for men and women, as well as make-up lessons for women to ensure their make-up complements their new look. Find your nearest consultants online and discuss holding a demonstration. Raise funds by charging an entrance fee, selling refreshments and adding a raffle or other fundraiser.

Give your funds a further boost after the event by asking your guests to clear out their wardrobes and hold a clothes exchange or 'swishing' party (see Clothes exchange) where they can exchange their unloved items for clothes and accessories in the colours and styles that suit them.

***

See also: How do I make it safe and legal?; Food safety; Licensing – playing live and recorded music and Lotteries and non-commercial gaming and betting.

8

New life for old

Second-hand goods are 'sold as seen' and if you're selling as a private individual you will be largely outside the controls of consumer law. However, you still need to ensure that goods are 'as described'. For example, a coat can't be a size 10 if it was described as a size 14. If you describe something as 'working', then it should be.

Some things simply aren't worth selling. Trading standards advise people not to buy second-hand child car seats, cycle helmets and riding hats unless they are buying from a friend or relative and are quite sure of their history. This is because involvement in an accident or simply dropping the item can affect the internal structure, even if any damage is not visible on the exterior.

If you, your charity or good cause, hold regular sales of second-hand items you may be regarded as a trader in the eyes of the law, in which case buyers are entitled to expect that any items sold are not only 'as described' but also of 'satisfactory quality' and 'fit for purpose'. Bear in mind that second-hand items will be judged less rigorously than new goods – buyers cannot expect used goods to be of the same quality as new products.

Take reasonable precautions – which means taking positive steps – to make sure that anything you sell is safe and meets any safety regulations which apply to that particular item. Be particularly careful with children's toys, electrical goods, upholstered furniture (such as cot mattresses, high chairs, buggies and prams), cosmetics and some children's clothing such as jackets or coats with drawstring necks.

Contact your local trading standards department or search your local authority website for product-specific information.

If you have any doubts about the safety of anything you have been given to sell, don't sell it. It's simply not worth any sleep you might lose – or the reputation of your organisation or good cause – if someone is hurt.

Out tray sale

Clear out your unwanted bric-a-brac and bring the money in by holding an out tray sale at work. Just put any items you no longer want or need in your out tray and move it to the end of your desk or somewhere nearby where your colleagues will walk past. Display your prices with information about the cause or charity you're supporting and whether you will be donating all, or a percentage of, the sale price.

Clothes exchange

Spring clean your wardrobe and recycle your old clothes by holding a clothes swapping or 'swishing' party.

Ask supporters to look out clothes and accessories which they no longer want, or which no longer fit. Set a minimum and maximum number of items which you want everyone to bring, which must be clean and ironed, and ideally on a hanger ready to be displayed.

It's important that donated clothes are in good condition. Shoes that you hoped would 'stretch to fit', or the outfit you bought which would be a perfect fit – if only you could lose a bit of weight – are ideal. Arrange them by size and type on clothes racks and display handbags, belts, jewellery, scarves and other accessories on tables.

Make sure your venue has suitable rooms where people can try on articles in private and make it clear to donors what will happen to any items left over at the end of the event.

Charge everyone an entrance fee of between £3 and £6, to include a number of tokens which they can swap for items of their choice. If there's a particularly desirable item, such as a designer dress or handbag, which a number of people want, hold a draw to avoid any tussles.

Once everyone has swapped all their tokens you can charge a flat price or take bids for any additional items they would like.

As well as exchanging clothes, you could swap CDs and DVDs. Make it into more of an occasion by offering light refreshments or adding a mini fashion parade at the start of the event.

Car boot, jumble and garage sales

Car boot sales are great to shift clutter. Ask everyone you know for their unwanted books, clothes, DVDs, ornaments, toys – anything that's in good enough condition to sell.

Read local newspapers and use the internet to search for local car boot sales (try www.carbootsales.org and www.carbootjunction.com).

Look at their rules, for instance the size of stalls, number of helpers allowed and any restrictions on what can be sold.

Put price tags on all your items before the sale or, if you're pushed for time, sort them into different boxes according to price bands, eg 50p, £1, £3, etc.

Take a table (picnic or decorating table); chairs for yourself and your helpers; an old rug or blanket to display items on the ground; a secure container with plenty of change (count your float beforehand so you can deduct it from the total amount raised); plenty of plastic bags; and something to eat and drink. Borrow some form of awning if there's a possibility of rain.

Car booters hunting for the best bargains (often to re-sell at the same event) will swarm around you as soon as you begin to unload. Keep your money box safe, and if you feel overwhelmed just lock your vehicle and get your remaining items out once they've left you in peace.

If you've plenty of help and a suitable venue, you might want to organise a jumble sale. If you're not sure you'll have enough items to sell, think about applying for a licence and organising a door-to-door collection.

An alternative is to hold a garage sale – less hassle – but success relies on plenty of publicity and a suitable location on a main road or area where there are plenty of people driving or walking by.

Make sure donors know what you plan to do with any unsold items. If your garage sale is within the boundaries of your own property you are unlikely to need a street trading licence or consent, but check with your local authority.

Nearly new sale

Nearly new sales of baby and children's clothing, toys and safety equipment are in demand; they're environmentally friendly, and a great way to engage the community.

Stair gates, sterilisers, high chairs, buggies and cots are expensive purchases and mums are likely to be reluctant to donate items which are in good condition which they could sell on eBay or by placing an advertisement in a local shop. The solution is to offer to sell the items for them in return for a commission (usually 20–30%) for your charity or good cause.

Spring and autumn are particularly good times to hold your event, enabling parents to buy or sell paddling pools and sand pits for the summer or warm coats and boots for the winter.

Allow yourself at least two months to plan your event, and bear in mind you will need plenty of helpers, both before and on the day itself. Most sales of this type run from late morning to mid-afternoon as you will need one to two hours to get everything ready before the doors open and a similar time afterwards to clear up and calculate your commission and your sellers' takings.

Advertise your sale in local businesses, shops, libraries, community centres, churches, schools, nurseries, doctors' surgeries and play groups.

Invite anyone who wants to bring items to sell to contact you or other nominated representatives before the event to register (name, address and contact details) and obtain a unique seller number and seller's pack. Ask sellers to attach a description of the item, the selling price and their number to each sale item and to deliver them in a box or boxes clearly marked with their registration number.

Make it clear in the seller's pack what you will and will not sell and that all items must be in good condition, fully working and meet any relevant safety regulations. Include copies of the safety standards for particular items (buggies, upholstered furniture, toys, electrical items, etc), or a link to where sellers can find the guidance on your local trading standards website, in the pack. Ask sellers to attach any instructions on use and intended age of the user to the relevant item, and, if they've lost the original instructions, to see if they can download a copy from the manufacturer's website.

Suggest sellers price goods sensibly and fairly – generally no more than a quarter to a third of the high street price – and set drop-off and pick-up times for boxes. Warn sellers that you will not be responsible if anything is damaged or lost and tell them how you intend to dispose of any unsold items which are not collected after the sale.

Run your own check on items on the day of the sale. If you have any doubts about anything offered for sale, don't sell it.

Make sure you have clothes rails and tables to display items on, plenty of loose change and bags for people to take their purchases home.

As items are sold, take the sellers' tickets off and keep them in a separate box. At the end of the sale sort the tickets by registration number so you have a pile for each seller. Calculate each seller's takings, minus your commission, and put the money and tickets from the sold items in an envelope with the seller's number on the front. Put unsold items back in the relevant numbered boxes supplied by the sellers. When sellers arrive to pick up their takings and any unsold goods, ask them for their number and check that their name and address tallies with the information on the registration form.

Charge a small entrance fee and add face painting or other activities for children as well as selling teas, coffees, squash, cones of children's sweets and homemade cakes.

Pop-up shop

Is there a shop near you which is vacant or you've heard is about to become vacant? Approach the landlord and ask if you can use the shop to sell donated goods. Alternatively, talk to your local planning authority about running a pop-up shop in a community hall or other venue.

Collect scrap gold

Gold and other precious metals, such as silver and platinum, are currently commanding high prices. Ask people to donate their broken chains, solitary earrings and other unwanted jewellery to help your cause.

A 9ct gold earring butterfly could raise £1.25 and if you've a gold tooth crown hanging around you could be filling your coffers by another £35. Get quotes from reputable jewellery shops and search online to get the best price per gram. The benefit of dealing with a jewellery shop is that the gold stays in your possession until you sell it and they will generally be able to tell you whether your item is gold or not and give you a quote straight away.

Online dealers will give you a quote based on the carat and weight of your items. You then send them the items for verification and receive an offer. Bear in mind that like any other commodity, gold prices can go up and down.

Recycle mobile phones

Many charities and organisations are already recycling old mobile phones in exchange for cash. Some are worth a tidy sum – particularly a top of the range model – others not as much. Ask supporters to have a rummage at home. They may well have perfectly usable phones lying unloved and out of sight in cupboards and drawers, simply because the charger has been lost, or they've upgraded to a newer model.

Old phones are sold to a new user or, if they can't be repaired, any rare metals are extracted and sold for scrap.

Use the internet to search for the best deal. Generally you'll need to supply details of the name and model of the phone and the phone recycling companies will quote you a price. If you accept their offer they will send you a bag or envelope for you to post them your phone and they will pay you the money once they've received it.

Advise your donors to make sure they transfer or delete all personal contacts and information, any security codes or passwords, and remove the SIM card.

Sell old ink cartridges

Recycling old printer ink cartridges makes sense as well as money. The average printer cartridge can be re-used several times but millions are dumped every year rather than being recycled.

The two main types of printer cartridges which can be recycled are laser cartridges (usually in larger, office printers) and the small inkjet or bubble jet cartridges found in home printers.

A number of national charities have set up printer cartridge recycling schemes with recycling companies. Supporters send the cartridges direct to the company and the charities receive a small amount of money for each one recycled.

Smaller organisations could set up collection points at school and nursery reception areas, churches or local shops where people can deposit their used cartridges. When you've collected enough they can be sent to, or collected by, a recycling company. As with mobile phone and gold recycling, it's important to shop around to find the best deal.

Whether you're collecting precious metals, mobile phones or ink cartridges, the important thing is to make sure as many people as possible know about it. Promote your recycling scheme in newsletters, on your website, and on posters and flyers.

Use your phone and cartridge collection boxes to provide information about your charity or good cause and explain how the proceeds will be used. Empty the boxes regularly and arrange regular recycling drives to remind people about the scheme.

***

See also: How do I make it safe and legal?; Street and door-to-door collections and Food safety.

9
Every penny counts

Street and door-to-door collections

If you want to collect money or sell articles in the street or other public place to benefit your charity or good cause, you will need to obtain a street collection permit from the relevant local authority, the Metropolitan Police (if you're collecting in Greater London) or your local police station in Northern Ireland.

The legislation governing street collections defines a street as 'any highway and any public bridge, road, lane, footway, square, court, alley or passage, whether a thoroughfare or not'. A 'public place' is defined as any place to which the public has access without payment, and this includes bus and railway stations, car parks, walkways in privately owned shopping centres and shop doorways.

Policies and regulations in regard to street collections vary according to the type of collection and the area where you want to collect. Always check with the relevant authority before carrying out a street collection to see whether or not a permit is required.

If you're planning to collect at a railway station, shopping centre or other place which is open to the public but on private property, you will also need permission from the owner or the individual who is responsible for the premises.

If you want to call door-to-door to collect money or items to sell at a jumble sale or pop-up shop, you will need to apply to the local authority for a door-to-door collection permit. Permits are issued free of charge, although you may be asked to pay an administration fee.

Pub-to-pub collections will need a door-to-door collection permit as well as permission from the licensees of the pubs you want to visit.

Apply for a permit as soon as possible prior to any collection – contact the relevant authority to find out their time frame for applications.

More than 40 charities hold a national exemption which means they do not have to obtain a licence for door-to-door collections. If you're collecting for a major charity, check with them first as they may well have an exemption.

The permit holder or 'promoter' is responsible for appointing and authorising collectors and ensuring any age limit and other conditions are complied with. Collection boxes must clearly show the cause or charity you are collecting for and be closed and sealed in such a way that they cannot be opened without breaking the seal.

You do not need a licence to have a static collection box in a pub, hotel, shop or business, just permission from the owner of the business.

Bottle of coins

Ask your local pub if they will let you have a large glass bottle or jar on their bar counter. Advertise your charity or good cause and how the money will be used on the bottle and invite everyone to donate their loose change. Make sure it's secure and tamper-proof. When the coins get near to the top of the bottle build a sense of excitement by holding a competition with a prize for who-ever can guess the number of coins or the amount of money which will be in the full bottle. Set a date with the licensee to open the bottle and discuss how you can turn it into an event in itself – perhaps by adding a disco, quiz or other fundraiser. Make sure there's a secure area where you can count the cash, and take plenty of coin bags.

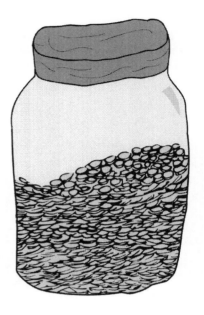

Mile of pennies

The UK penny has a diameter of 20.3mm, that's 79,278 pennies in a mile – and £792.78 for your charity or cause.

The original idea of laying pennies end-to-end in a street or school playground (think of the logistics!) has evolved into challenging as many supporters as possible to fill a drink can or similar-sized container with coins with the aim of collecting enough to make a mile.

Keep your contributors informed about how the challenge is progress-ing and encourage them to keep going until you reach your target. Try and collect the tins and bank your pennies in batches. Each penny weighs 3.56 grams. If you collect 100,000, that's the weight of a small car to store and transport!

Coin challenge

Decide what distance you think you can cover with coins, depending on the time available, the number of helpers and the venue. Invite people to lay down as many coins as they feel able to help you to reach your target. This can be run as an individual activity or part of a bigger event. Don't forget health and safety considerations – place coins in an area where they will be obvious and less likely to cause slippages – and check whether you'll need a street collection permit.

Collection boxes

How about having your own, unique collection box – maybe in the shape of the new building you're fundraising for, a tent for the Guide group or a children's play house to represent the play equipment you want to provide for your school or playgroup? Source a supplier online or recruit a graphic designer to do it for you. Ensure the boxes are tamper-proof and ask local shops and businesses if they would lend their support by putting them on their counters.

Coins in Smarties tubes

Every little helps. And little people like to help too! Ask people to support your cause by giving out Smarties tubes and encouraging youngsters to fill them with 1p or 20p coins and adults with 20p or £1 coins – once they've emptied them of sweets!

Bucket collection

Always give well-wishers who attend your events and are willing to support your cause, but don't necessarily want to take part in the activities, the opportunity to make a donation via a well-secured bucket or tin.

Shopping affiliate schemes

What if you could raise money by simply shopping at your favourite stores? Well you can – it's called affiliate shopping.

Every time your supporters buy from selected online retailers, which include John Lewis, Tesco, Marks & Spencer and Amazon, the stores will make a donation to your charity, club, community group or school – and it won't cost your supporters a penny extra.

If the cause you are seeking to support is not already registered, fill in the online registration form giving your contact details and where to send the money raised – which is paid direct to your cause. Once your application has been approved start your publicity and watch your funds grow.

Find out more by visiting www.giveasyoulive.com or www.easyfundraising.org.uk.

Supermarket bag packing

Depending on the size of the supermarket, the number of customers and the number of helpers you can enrol, bag packing at supermarkets can raise hundreds of pounds. There's plenty of competition to fundraise in this way so you'll need to be flexible when discussing dates (usually weekends) with your local stores. Make the most of the opportunity by giving your helpers advice on how to approach customers to see if they need help and showing them how to pack (eggs and lettuce are best at the top, rather than the bottom, of the bag!).

Take plenty of publicity material explaining why you are raising money as some shoppers might want to do their own packing but would be willing to make a donation. Grab shoppers' attention by wearing uniforms or T-shirts with the name of the charity or good cause you're supporting. Write to the store afterwards to thank them and let them know how much you raised.

***

See also: How do I make it safe and legal?

10

Lotteries and non-commercial gaming and betting

Lotteries

Lotteries are well-loved fundraisers because they're so adaptable. Prizes can be tailored to suit different age groups, interests and events – for example handmade items at a craft fair; hampers of food, champagne and weekends away at a black tie dinner; or teddies and toys at a nursery or pre-school fun day.

Whether lotteries – which include raffles and tombolas – are run for fun or to fundraise, they're a form of gambling. Bear in mind that some organisations don't approve of lotteries for this reason and some people will not sell or buy tickets.

The law covering gambling in England, Wales and Scotland is set out in the Gambling Act 2005 and subsidiary legislation, and is regulated by the Gambling Commission.

The regulations governing lotteries in Northern Ireland are more restrictive than in England, Wales and Scotland. Information on running charity lotteries and other fundraisers involving gambling in Northern Ireland is available from the Social Policy Unit at the Department for Social Development. The information in this chapter relates specifically to England, Wales and Scotland.

The first step is to establish what kind of lottery you want to run and whether you will need permission from your local authority or the Gambling Commission. This will be determined by where and when you want to sell the tickets, and who you plan to sell tickets to. You will be able to get further guidance and information from the licensing officer at your local authority or the Gambling Commission website.

Despite the rules and regulations, lotteries are generally easy to set up and cheap to run – particularly if you can persuade people to donate prizes.

All prizes have to be allocated, even if you are unable to generate sufficient ticket sales to cover your expenses, so try to avoid spending money on prizes. Approach local businesses, as well as your supporters, and ask if they would be willing to supply a prize. Tailor each letter to the individual business and offer to mention them in your publicity.

Under the licensing laws alcohol must not be awarded to anyone under the age of 18 (it would be considered supplying alcohol to a minor). Another prize of equal value could be given instead. Alcohol offered as prizes must be in sealed containers and under 18s can only sell tickets if they are supervised by an adult. The law in Northern Ireland prohibits the sale of alcohol without a licence and fundraisers could be committing an offence if they offer alcohol as lottery prizes unless licensed to do so.

Incidental non-commercial lottery

You don't need to get permission to run a lottery at a non-commercial event such as a village fair or at a social event such as a lunch for older people, as long as you stick to the rules.

- The lottery must be incidental to the event and not the main event or the main reason for people to attend the event.
- All proceeds, once money spent on prizes and the cost of running the lottery have been deducted, must be used for charitable purposes or to support sport, athletics or other non-commercial activity.
- Tickets can only be sold at and during the event, not before.
- No more than £500 can be spent on prizes, but donated gifts don't count towards this.
- The organiser cannot claim more than £100 from the proceeds for the costs of running the lottery, even if it has cost more.
- The draw must be made, and the winners announced, during the event.
- All raffle prizes which have been offered have to be won, even if ticket sales haven't covered your expenses or the cost of the prizes.
- The lottery cannot involve a rollover of prizes from one lottery to another.

Raffle and tombola tickets are the only lottery tickets that can be sold at a discount, for instance 50p per ticket but £2 for a strip of five. Likewise, if you still have tombola prizes left near the end of the event, there are no restrictions on reducing the price of tickets in order to sell them.

Tombolas

A few weeks before your event ask supporters to donate prizes. This will give you enough time to see if you need to buy any prizes, particularly the crowd pullers such as wine or boxes of chocolates. Decide what proportion of tickets will be winners, depending on how many prizes you have. Most tombolas award prizes for ticket numbers ending in a five and a nought. Tear out tickets ending in a five or nought (or whatever you've chosen) and attach them to your prizes. Fold the counterfoils and put them in a tombola drum or large bucket. Cloakroom tickets, which can be bought from most stationery stores, are ideal. Next, pull out the losing tickets, leaving the counterfoils in the book, fold them and add them to your drum or bucket. Decide how much you want to sell the tickets for. On the day of the tombola make your prizes look as attractive as possible by arranging them on a table or display unit, giving pride of place to your main prizes.

Soft toy tombola

Ask children, and their parents, to donate teddies and other soft toys. You are likely to be overwhelmed by cuddly bears, dogs, rabbits, pandas and other toys.

Make sure they are all clean, safe and suitable to have on your tombola. Then give them each a number, or even a name. Attach the ticket number or name to each toy and put the duplicates, along with the losing tickets, in the tombola tub.

You may have enough toys to award a prize each time; if not, buy a stock of small lollies or sweets so no child walks away empty handed.

Balloon tombola

Buy a good stock of balloons of different colours. Prepare a slip of paper for each balloon, either awarding a prize or saying something like 'Sorry, you haven't won this time' or 'Have another go!' Tightly fold the papers, inflate the balloons and insert a paper into each balloon before you tie the neck. Entrants burst their chosen balloon to see if they've won a prize.

Beer glass tombola

Ask people to donate bottles of wine or buy them from a super-market or off-licence – look out for offers! Decide on the ratio of wine to winning tickets and put the folded tombola tickets in a beer glass. Anyone who draws a winning number wins a bottle of wine. This type of tombola is quick, easy to run and ideal for an evening event. It would work equally well, depending on the type of event, with chocolates or other prizes. If it's a big event, you could have a number of beer glasses and volunteers who can circulate among the guests between courses or during any interval. Make sure any-one who plays is aged 18 or over as under 18s must not be given alcohol as a prize.

Private lotteries

If you are fundraising for a club, society or other group, you can also run a 'private society lottery' without a licence, provided:

- the club has not been set up for gambling
- the promoter is an authorised member of the society
- tickets are only advertised and sold to society members or peo-ple on premises wholly or mainly used for the administration of the society
- all the proceeds are spent on prizes and/or the purposes for which the society is run
- tickets show the name and address of the promoter, the ticket price, any restrictions on who may, or may not, buy a ticket and that tickets are non-transferable
- the price of tickets is the same for everyone (but there is no restriction on how much you can charge for tickets)
- prizes are not 'rolled over' from one lottery to another.

122

100 clubs

Named after how many people are taking part, 100 clubs are a form of private society lottery (see main requirements). A tried and tested way of securing a regular monthly income, they work particularly well for school Parent Teacher Associations (PTAs), sports clubs and uniformed groups. The idea is to recruit a set number of players (it could be 100 or, if it's a small society or group, 50 or 25) to pay a monthly or annual subscription for a number which is entered into a monthly draw.

The group agrees what percentage of this money (less expenses) goes to the group's funds and how much is awarded in prizes (generally 55% to the group and 45% for prize money).

Agree in advance how long each player will hold their number (for instance from September to August for school PTAs or January to December for other groups). Encourage players to pay by direct debit or standing order to reduce the administration.

Before making the draw the administrator checks that all members have paid and then draws the winning number(s) at random. It's good practice to do this in front of one or two other people or at a club meeting or event.

Remember that to keep within the legislation, only members of the society or group can take part.

Small and large society lotteries – 'prize draws'

A lottery where tickets are sold to members of the public in advance of the draw is called a 'society lottery'.

If the total value of the tickets is less than £20,000, it is classed as a 'small society lottery' and you will need to register with the local authority (Licensing Board in Scotland). There is an annual fee which is reduced if you re-register for a second year.

If you expect to sell tickets with a face value of more than £20,000, the lottery is a 'large society lottery' and you will need to apply for a licence from the Gambling Commission. It's important to seek advice early if you're planning to run a society lottery.

Once again, there are a number of rules you'll need to follow.

- Your society must be set up for non-commercial purposes, eg sports, cultural or charitable.
- The tickets must show the name of the society, the name and address of the promoter, the price of the ticket, when the draw will take place and any other information required by the local authority or Gambling Commission.
- At least 20% of the proceeds must go to the charity or good cause the lottery is supporting. This means that up to 80% can be spent on prizes and expenses.
- The maximum prize in a single small society lottery is £25,000. For a large society lottery, it is £25,000 or 10% of the gross ticket sales, whichever is the greater.
- The maximum value of tickets that can be sold in a single large society lottery is £4m.
- There is no maximum ticket price but all tickets must be sold at the same price.
- Tickets can be sold in a kiosk or shop, or door-to-door (provided a door-to-door collection permit has been granted by the local authority). They cannot be sold in the street or at any kind of gambling establishment.
- Tickets cannot be sold by, or to, people aged under 16.

- Rollovers are allowed, provided the maximum single prize limit is not breached.

If you want to run a small or large society lottery, approach stores, hotel chains, travel firms and local businesses and ask if they would consider donating or offering a generous discount on electrical goods, holidays, weekend breaks, food hampers or any other prizes you think would appeal to your target market.

Shop around for a printer who can offer the best deal. Each ticket will need a unique number and perforations to separate the ticket from the stub. Advertise the top prizes on the tickets and make sure you include all the details required by the terms of the licence or registration. Recruit as many people as possible to sell tickets and consider offering an incentive, such as a prize, to whoever sells the most tickets. Record the names of everyone to whom you have distributed tickets to sell, along with their unique ticket numbers.

Why not make the draw itself a fundraiser by announcing where and when it will take place and providing drinks and light refreshments? If you have a particularly high value item invite a local VIP to present the prize to the winner at a suitable time and place and invite the local media along or send them a picture.

Whenever and wherever you're running any sort of lottery it's essential that you conduct the draw in such a way that everyone can be confident that it has been done fairly and legally. Ask someone who has not purchased a ticket to do the draw or blindfold a random participant and ask them to select the winners. If you are offering a number of prizes, announce which prize is being allocated before that ticket is drawn. Keep a record of who has won which prizes and make it available to anyone who asks for it. Where possible, publish the winning numbers and/or winners on your website.

Once the lottery has been held you'll need to supply details, including how much you collected, and how much you spent on expenses and prizes. Keep accurate records of the proceeds and how much you spent (with receipts), who donated prizes, the amount allotted to your charity or good cause and the number of sold and unsold tickets.

Scratch cards

Scratch cards are printed cards with small panels that are covered with a special coating. Contestants scratch the coating off and win a prize if they uncover a specified number of matching symbols or amounts of cash. You'll have seen the National Lottery scratch cards on sale at shops and filling stations – but have you ever considered selling your own?

Search online to find a company which offers different scratch cards for charities and good causes. Choose one which is able to personalise your card with the name of your charity and, where possible, add brief information about how any money raised will be used.

Ask local traders if they would be willing to sell the cards on your behalf, either to support your cause or for a small commission. Sell them to friends and family, and ask supporters to take them to work to sell to colleagues. Have them available at other events when you're raising money for your community, group or other good cause. As you'll be selling the scratch cards to the general public over a period of time, scratch card fundraisers are classed as society lotteries and you'll need to register with your local authority (Licensing Board in Scotland).

Another type of scratch card fundraiser is where players buy a name or numbered square on a larger card and write their contact details on their chosen square. Once all the squares have been sold the winner's box is scratched off to reveal the lucky name or number. This type of scratch card fundraiser is usually run as part of a bigger charity event such as a fun day or pub sports day. If only people at the event can buy squares and the winner will be revealed during the event, it is an incidental non-commercial lottery.

Duck race

Duck races are another form of lottery. Participants 'buy' a rubber or plastic duck for £1, £2 or whatever sum you choose. The number or name of the duck is written in waterproof ink or paint on each duck. Once all the ducks have been sold they are released into a stream or river. The first duck over the finishing line wins the race and its owner wins the prize.

Because buying a duck is the equivalent of buying a lottery ticket, you'll need to follow the rules for a small (or large) society lottery if you plan to sell tickets in advance of the race day.

The size of the race will depend on how many ducks you think you can sell and the space and availability of a suitable stretch of water – ideally a slow moving stream or river which is easily accessible with no obstacles to impede the ducks.

You'll need to get the permission of the owner of any stretch of water that you plan to race on. In the case of public parks, this is likely to be the local authority. The local water or river authority should be able to help identify private owners. Make sure there is enough room for people to gather at the start and finish of the race. You will also need to arrange a boom or other trap to catch the ducks at the end of the race as well as nets to scoop the race finishers out of the water and to rescue any ducks which were trapped along the route.

Because of the risks posed by running water you will need to be ultra safety conscious. Ensure you have adequate public liability insurance and do a thorough risk assessment. Take any safety measures which may be required such as putting up barriers, roping off areas that are, or could become, slippery or hazardous, appointing marshals to ensure that spectators – particularly children – don't get too close to the water and having first aiders or medics on hand. The owners of the water may also want to impose conditions.

Balloon race

Balloon releases and balloon races have long been a way for charities, schools and businesses to fundraise or to mark an important event. But they're now dropping out of favour due to concerns that the balloon remains are harming birds and marine life.

As with duck races, balloon races are classed as lotteries. Buying a balloon is like buying a lottery ticket and you'll need to register with the local authority or obtain a licence from the Gambling Commission in order to sell tickets before the race day.

The idea is that people buy a helium-filled balloon which is attached to a card with their name and information about how the finder can return the card and claim a prize. The balloons are then released and the owner of the card that is returned from the farthest distance by a fixed date wins the race.

A number of wildlife and animal charities are campaigning against intentional balloon releases. They say birds become tangled up in the balloon ribbon and are unable to fly and sea animals mistake the balloon fragments for food and eat them. The balloon can then block their guts, causing them to starve to death.

Dozens of local authorities have now banned balloon releases on their land and are discouraging organisations within their area from holding them. A number of major organisations have also stated that they will no longer support balloon releases.

Why raise money for one good cause only to cause problems for another? How about building a balloon sculpture instead? As it's not a lottery, you won't need a licence. Ask supporters to buy balloons but then use the balloons to build a sculpture. The balloon companies have risen to the challenge by providing instructions for making balloon arches and selling assembly materials. You could even hire a balloon artist to create something unusual and eye-catching. Try and obtain sponsorship for the event and see if you can attract a celebrity to attach the first or final balloon. Encourage supporters to drop in to check on progress and add to your funds by providing refreshments and other activities such as a balloon tombola.

***

For more information about running any kind of lottery, visit the lotteries section on the Gambling Commission website (see Useful contacts and resources).

The government is planning to lift some of the restrictions on incidental non-commercial lotteries and other smaller lotteries. If you are planning to hold any form of lottery visit the Gambling Commission website to check you have the most up-to-date information (Social Policy Unit, Department for Social Development in Northern Ireland).

***

Non-commercial gaming and betting

Charity casino evenings, race nights and bingo are classed as 'non-commercial gaming' and can be run without a licence or any other form of permit, as long as you comply with the rules. Gaming can be an incidental activity or the only or principal purpose of the event – as long as none of the proceeds are used for private gain.

Some charities and good causes do not approve of gambling, so you might want to check with a representative of the body you're fundraising for before you start planning this type of event.

There are two types of non-commercial gaming – prize gaming and equal chance gaming. Choose which you think is most suitable for your event and the people you hope to attract.

While some premises restrict entry to people aged 18 and over, there are no age limits for non-commercial prize or equal chance gaming, although you could set what you consider to be a suitable minimum age limit for your event.

Prize gaming

In prize gaming, prizes must be decided and advertised before the game starts. Prizes can be cash, goods or services, but their nature and size must not be dependent on the number of people playing or the amount of money staked.

There are no statutory limits on stakes, prizes, participation fees or other charges for this type of gaming, which means it's a good option for fundraisers. Again, there are rules to follow.

- Players must be told that the purpose of the gaming is to raise money for a specific charity or good cause, and which charity or good cause will benefit, before play begins.
- All the proceeds (minus reasonable costs from organising the event and money spent on prizes) must go to your charity or good cause. This includes entrance and participation fees, money raised by sponsorship, and commission or fees from traders. (Money raised by other people – for instance refreshments provided by an independent third party – does not form part of the proceeds and can be kept by that third party.)
- The gaming must be in person, on premises and cannot be remote.
- There are restrictions on holding non-commercial prize gaming events at licensed gambling premises and race tracks. (Visit the Gambling Commission website for further information.)

Equal chance gaming

In equal chance gaming everyone has an equal chance of winning and players are not competing against a bank. This includes games such as poker and bingo. The amount or value of prizes varies according to the number of participants and/or the money they stake.

- You must tell players that the purpose of the gaming is to raise money for a specific charity or good cause, and which charity or good cause will benefit, before play begins.
- All of the proceeds (minus reasonable costs from organising the event and money spent on prizes) must go to your charity or good cause. This includes entrance and participation fees, money raised by sponsorship, and commission or fees from traders. (Money raised by other people – for instance refreshments provided by an independent third party – does not form part of the proceeds and may be kept for private gain.)

- The maximum amount a player can be charged is £8 per day. This includes entrance or participation fees, stakes and any other payments in relation to the gaming. (The £8 limit applies to the gaming element and would not include any payment for refreshments.)
- The total amount or value of prizes must not exceed £600 in total across all players. The maximum amount includes both money and the monetary value of goods, vouchers, donated items and goodybags. A higher prize fund is permitted if the game is the final one of a series in which all the players have previously taken part.
- The gaming must be in person, on premises and cannot be remote.
- There are restrictions on holding non-commercial equal chance gaming events at licensed gambling premises and race tracks. (Visit the Gambling Commission website for further information.)

Fun casino evening

Ready to roll? Dust off the dinner jacket or little black dress and try your luck with a casino evening.

Never been inside a casino? Don't worry! There are a number of professional casino providers who will run the event for you and supply everything you need, from the croupiers and tables to the chips and fun money. A casino provider is likely to charge a starting price of between £300 and £400 for two tables – roulette and blackjack being the most prevalent casino games. The more tickets you expect to sell, the more tables you'll need.

Once you've chosen a supplier and venue, consider whether you want to have a theme. Suitable themes include James Bond, gangsters and molls, and black and white. Think about whether you want to provide a sit-down meal, hot or cold buffet, canapés or just nibbles. This will largely depend on what theme you choose and how much you want to charge. Work out how much you want to raise, how much you need to cover your expenses and how many tickets you think you will be able to sell. This will give you your minimum ticket price. The tickets are likely to be your main source of income, so publicise your event as widely as possible and recruit volunteers to sell tickets in advance.

Try and cover the costs of the casino equipment and staff by finding at least one sponsor for each table.

Give guests an initial stake of chips or fun money as part of their entrance fee. It should be enough for guests to feel they've received value for money and enable conservative players to play throughout the event. Offer the option of buying additional chips or fun money if players lose their initial stake.

Guests will expect to be able to have a drink while they play, so consider whether you want to provide alcohol yourself, find a venue with a licensed bar, or invite guests to bring a bottle and charge corkage.

Find the winning punters by counting who has the most casino chips or fun money at the end of the night and present them with their prizes.

Casino nights can also be run as equal chance gaming. In this case organisers need to be careful to ensure that no player spends more than £8 (to include the entrance fee and any additional purchase of chips or fun money) and that no more than £600 is paid out in prizes.

Race night

There are plenty of winners at a race night – including your charity or good cause.

Instead of standing by the track, baking in the sun or shivering in the cold, why not organise your own night at the races in the comfort of your local school, church or community hall?

Participants in a charity race night stake money on the outcome of pre-recorded races which are projected onto a large screen. The selection of a horse is totally dependent on chance and there are no 'odds' or 'form' to aid a player's choice. There are usually six to nine races with eight horses in each race. Players pick a horse they want to back from the race programme.

Most race nights attract between 50 and 80 people but large ones can have as many as 200 guests or more. Make sure you choose a venue with enough space for people to sit and move about to place bets. Check whether the venue has equipment to screen the races or if not, whether you can bring your own screen and DVD player. Test the equipment beforehand to make sure it works. As you will be show-ing films, be sure to check that this is covered in the venue's premises licence or club premises certificate. If not, you will need to serve a Temporary Event Notice on the local authority (apply for a Temporary Public Entertainment Licence in Scotland).

It's important to choose the right master of ceremonies. Ideally this should be someone who can build a rapport with the race goers, ener-gise the room and get everyone settled and back from the bar!

There are a number of companies which will run the event for you or provide a basic package to include DVDs of genuine races run in the past, betting slips, templates for producing your own race cards and instructions on how to run the evening.

Once you've decided the number of races, approach local businesses to see if they would be willing to sponsor a race – which they could name – and provide prizes for the owners of the winning horse and jockey in their race. Try and sell the horses and jockeys in all of the races except the final one to an owner who will be there on the night. The owners get a chance to name their horse or jockey and receive a prize if they win. Start approaching prospective sponsors and owners as early as possible to give them the opportunity of having their names and the name of their race, horse or jockey in the race programme.

The last race is generally an auction race where each horse and jockey is sold to the highest bidder, with bigger prizes to be won by the owners of the winning horse and jockey.

How much you charge for each bet is your decision and will depend on what you think your guests can afford, but it's generally 50p or £1. Once everyone has picked a horse and placed their bets a member of the audience is asked to select a race from a selection of unmarked DVDs. Once the race has been played, award prizes to people who backed the winner and to the owners of the winning horse and jockey.

You could award the smaller prizes after each race and present the bigger prizes for owners at the end of the evening as a grand finale.

Encourage guests to dress up for the occasion – the more hats the merrier! You could even award prizes for the most amazing headgear and best dressed man and woman.

Charge an admission fee and increase your takings by selling refreshments and adding other fundraising activities.

A race night can also be held as non-commercial equal chance gaming. First of all, decide the percentage you will retain for your charity or good cause. Explain to guests at the start of your event that you will be using a betting tote system to calculate the winnings in each race. A betting tote system works by collecting all the bets before the race. The agreed percentage of money staked is retained for the charity or good cause and the remainder is divided between the players who have backed the winning horse. For instance, if you sell 100 bets at £1 each and keep 50% for fundraising, that leaves £50 for prize money.

Once the tote is closed the master of ceremonies announces the race and the betting tote staff quickly calculate the prize money. If 20 people have backed the winning horse, they will share the prize money, each winning £2.50. Similarly, if you sell each horse in a race for £5, that's £40. Keep £20 (50%) for your charity and award £20 to the winning owner. The tote is then re-opened for the next race and the whole process is repeated until the final race has been run.

Take care to ensure that no more than £600 is paid out in prizes and that no player pays more than £8 per day in entrance or participation fees, stakes or any other payments in relation to the gaming.

Bingo

Bingo is sociable, fun and easy to play. A bingo caller selects a random number, usually on a tile or small ball, from a bag, or uses a bingo machine which selects numbered balls. Each player has a card containing a set amount of numbers. The bingo caller calls out the selected number and if it matches a number on their card, players cross out that number, or cover it with a counter or piece of card. The first person to cross off all the numbers on their card (a full house) wins the game.

Most charity bingo events are played for the fun of it so you don't need to spend a lot on prizes. Bottles of wine (over 18s only), boxes of chocolates, store vouchers or donated goods or services could be offered as prizes for a full house. Smaller items such as promotional pens, bugs or magnets – if you have them, or bags of sweets if you don't – would be acceptable prizes for 'line' (first to complete a row on their card) or 'corners' (all four corners) games.

Bingo cards can be purchased at stationers or online. You could even design and print your own, which you could personalise with details about your good cause. Ask your local village hall or sports club if they have any bingo equipment you could borrow. Make sure you've plenty of pens or card 'markers' on the tables.

The star of the show will be your bingo caller. Look for someone with presence and a good sense of humour who can mug up on the 'bingo lingo'. There's a rhyme or phrase for every number (which you can find online), such as 'Kelly's eye' (number one) and 'two little ducks' (number 22). Find the caller an assistant who can keep a record of the numbers called during each game and help the caller to check the winning cards.

An average game will take about 15 minutes. Work out a plan of how many games you want to play, the variety of games and when you want to break for refreshments. Be flexible in case you have to drop or add on games if your timing goes askew on the night.

Consider including a hot supper such as fish and chips, pizza or chilli con carne. Suggest guests bring a bottle or run your own bar and sell soft drinks, tea and coffee. You could charge an all-in fee to include a card for every game or charge per game. Give players the option of increasing their chances – and the takings – by buying extra cards.

Decide whether your bingo event will be prize gaming or equal chance gaming and follow the appropriate rules.

***

The regulations governing lotteries and non-commercial gaming and betting are complex. The information in this book does not cover every detail of the legislation or constitute legal advice. If you are planning to hold any form of lottery or event involving gaming or betting, always check on the Gambling Commission website to make sure you are getting the most up-to-date information (Social Policy Unit, Department for Social Development in Northern Ireland).

Organisers are encouraged to get their own legal advice to ensure their plans comply with the law.

***

See also: How do I make it safe and legal?; Alcohol (liquor) licensing; Food safety; Licensing – playing live and recorded music and Sponsorship.

11
Special days and dates

There's a host of special dates throughout the year which offer opportunities for fundraising. Look out for awareness dates, special sporting or political events and historic anniversaries which you can link your fundraising to for extra fun and additional publicity.

New Year's Day

Get your fundraising year off to a good start by pledging to stop doing something (for instance smoking, swearing, etc) or to start doing something (walking to work, losing weight, etc) from 1 January. Ask your friends, relatives and colleagues to support and sponsor you.

Burns' night

Hold a Burns' night supper to celebrate the life and poetry of Robert Burns, on or near the poet's birthday on 25 January.

No longer the preserve of the Scots, Burns' night suppers can be a formal affair, or something a little less formal, but Scotland's national dish, the haggis, usually takes pride of place. The main ingredients for the evening's entertainment typically consist of the haggis – cut with a flourish using a ceremonial knife and traditionally served with mashed potatoes (tatties) and turnips (neeps) – whisky (Scotch of course!) and the recitation of Burns' poetry.

At a formal dinner the bagpipes feature large and the haggis is piped in by bagpipes, but if you want a more informal event, choose contemporary music. Setting a dress code can also help to get people into the swing of things, so you might want to encourage guests to wear something tartan.

You'll find the running order for a Burns' night celebration and the words of the Selkirk Grace and the poet's famous *Address to a Haggis* online. For more information search 'Burns night' on the BBC website (www.bbc.co.uk) or Wikipedia (www.en.wikipedia.org).

If you want to put a modern twist on things why not serve alternative Scottish produce such as smoked salmon or Aberdeen beef? See St Andrew's Day for typical Scottish fare.

Round off the evening with some light entertainment – a spot of traditional Scottish dancing, a rendition of Burns' poetry, or perhaps a whisky cocktail-making demonstration and tasting.

Valentine's Day

St Valentine, the patron saint of love, died on 14 February. Very little is known about St Valentine, but legend suggests he was a priest who was executed for performing marriages in secret in defiance of an edict outlawing marriage.

Another legend tells how, while he was in prison, he sent letters to his friends asking to be prayed for, saying 'Remember your Valentine'.

Put some romance into your fundraising.

- **Hold a Valentine's Day bake sale.** Bake cupcakes and decorate them with pink icing, red hearts, sugar roses, etc. Bake and decorate biscuits in the shape of hearts. Sell them at work, school, college or university.
- **Make and sell Valentine cards.**
- **Ask people to sponsor you to dress from head to toe in bright red for the day.**
- **Show a romantic movie.**
- **Host a Valentine disco or dance.**
- **Stage a picnic box auction.**
- **Organise a pamper evening or party.**

St David's Day

St David's Day is celebrated on 1 March in honour of St David (Dewi Sant), the patron saint of Wales. A renowned teacher and preacher, he helped spread Christianity across Wales.

Daffodils and leeks are regarded as the national emblems of Wales and are traditionally worn on St David's Day. The leek arises from an incident on the eve of battle when St David advised the Welsh to wear leeks in their caps so they could distinguish friend from foe.

- **Hold a concert with a male voice choir.**
- **Invite a harpist to perform.**
- **Ask colleagues to sponsor you to don the Welsh national costume on St David's Day.** Ladies wear a long woollen skirt, white blouse, woollen shawl and a tall black hat worn over a white

frilled bonnet. Men wear a white shirt, black waistcoat, black trousers, long woollen socks and black shoes.

- **Bake Welsh cakes and bara brith (a spicy fruit loaf) and sell them at work or arrange a Welsh coffee morning or afternoon tea.**
- **Serve traditional Welsh food.** Cawl, a Welsh stew, nowadays made with lamb and leeks, is recognised as the national dish of Wales. Baked trout and bacon, and roast lamb are also excellent choices. Finish the meal with apple cake and cream or a fruit pudding followed by Caerphilly cheese and biscuits.
- **Hold a meat-free meal.** (St David was a renowned vegetarian and refused to eat meat.) Glamorgan sausages – Caerphilly cheese and leeks shaped into sausages and coated in breadcrumbs – are another well-established dish.

Shrove Tuesday

Shrove Tuesday – better known to many as Pancake Day – is the last day before Lent, which is traditionally a time when Christians practise self-discipline by giving something up in recognition of the 40 days and nights which Jesus Christ spent in the desert without food.

In bygone times, Shrove Tuesday was the last chance for people to indulge themselves and use up any foods such as butter, eggs and sugar, which were not allowed during Lent, hence the association with pancakes.

The date of Shrove Tuesday is determined by Easter, which marks the end of Lent, and varies from year to year.

- **Ask friends and colleagues to sponsor you to give something up, or do something extra during Lent.**
- **Hold a pancake race.**

142

- **Invite people to your home for a crêpe supper.**
- **Play lemon roll.** Place a large lemon in a glass bowl and challenge people to balance a coin on top of the lemon. Award a prize or offer to double their money if they succeed and keep the coin when they don't.

St Patrick's Day

St Patrick, the patron saint of Ireland, was born in Britain but was captured by pirates and taken to Ireland as a slave. He eventually escaped back to Britain, where he trained as a cleric before returning to Ireland as a Christian missionary. St Patrick's Day (17 March) is a celebration of his life and Irish culture. Green clothing and green ribbons, which symbolise the Emerald Isle's lush greenery, are worn along with shamrocks which legend has it that St Patrick used to explain the Holy Trinity.

- **Hold a coffee morning or tea party.** Bake cupcakes with green icing, brownies with green frosting and barmbrach (a soft, spicy bread containing dried fruit). Take them to work to sell to colleagues or invite friends to tuck in and make a donation to your cause or charity.
- **Irish country dancing.** Invite a group to perform an Irish dance or hire a 'caller' to give your guests a lesson in Irish dancing.
- **Serve a feast of Irish food.** Lay on your own spread or team up with a local pub or restaurant. Serve a scrumptious menu of Irish favourites such as potato soup and soda bread, Irish stew or lamb shoulder, shepherd's pie, colcannon and fresh fruit and cream. Don't forget the stout!
- **Hold a whiskey tasting.** Team up with a local pub or hotel to sample a range of Irish whiskeys.
- **Four-leaf shamrock hunt.** Place pictures of three- and four-leaf shamrocks on a tray and cover each one with an egg shell or

143

plastic milk bottle top. Charge guests to uncover one of the shamrocks. Anyone who finds a four-leaf shamrock wins a small prize.

Easter

Christians celebrate the resurrection of Jesus Christ on Easter Sunday. The actual date of Easter changes every year (it is determined by the first Sunday following a full moon on or after 21 March) and can fall on any date between 22 March and 25 April.

Many families can enjoy a long weekend together and will be looking for things to do, which makes it an ideal time to hold a craft fair, scarecrow trail or other event.

How about organising a charity Easter egg hunt, Easter bonnet competition or cake sale? Bake Easter biscuits, Simnel cakes (a light fruitcake with layers of marzipan), chocolate cornflake nests (complete with mini eggs), egg and rabbit shaped biscuits and Easter cupcakes to sell to friends and colleagues.

St George's Day

St George – the dragon slayer – is the patron saint of England and his day is celebrated on 23 April. A soldier in the Roman army, he was executed for his faith after declaring himself a Christian and vociferously opposing an edict that all Christian soldiers should be arrested.

According to legend, a dragon made a nest in a spring where the townspeople collected water. In order to lure the dragon away they offered a sheep, and when no sheep could be found, a maiden. Lots were drawn to choose the victim and one day this happened to be the monarch's daughter. St George came across the scene on his travels, killed the dragon and rescued the princess.

- **Slay a few dragons.** Set up a team of dragon slayers to offer to do gardening, ironing, decorating, cleaning and other beastly tasks in return for a donation.
- **Serve a full English breakfast.** What better way to start the celebrations than with a tasty English breakfast at your home, church hall, local pub or cafe?
- **Serve a roast dinner or hold a hog roast.**
- **Arrange an English cream tea.**
- **Morris dancing.** Book a 'side', or 'team', of Morris dancers. Book early – St George's Day is a busy time for Morris dancers. Lay on some food or link up with a local pub.
- **Stage a mummers' play.** Mummers' plays are seasonal folk plays which date back to the mid 18th century but are thought to be much older. The principal characters vary regionally but are normally a hero – generally St George – a villain and a comical quack doctor who is called in to revive the villain. Contact a local troupe to see if they can help.
- **Hold an evening of folk music.**
- **Organise an archery display or competition with a local archery group.** (English archers were once feared for their prowess on the battlefield.)
- **Arrange a darts tournament.** The long-established pub game was created by English archers throwing arrow heads at the bottom of beer barrels.
- **Stage a dragon trail.** Run the trail on similar lines to a scarecrow trail.
- **Host a quiz night.** Think up questions about all things English. (See Fun quiz.)

Harvest

Harvest has traditionally been a time for communities – landowners, farmers and farm workers – to get together to celebrate a successful harvest and to eat, drink and generally make merry. Fewer people these days earn their living from the land, but the idea of celebrating harvest endures.

Your supper could range from a get-together of people who work on the same allotments or a shared picnic to a large event at a church or community hall. Try to use seasonal and locally-grown fruit and vegetables. Decorate the tables with tablecloths and napkins in autumnal colours and arrange flowers, fruit and vegetables on windowsills and tables.

Why not add a barn dance, invite a horticulturist to give a talk or hold a craft exhibition to show off the skill and creativity of people within your community?

Charge people for tickets and raise extra funds with a bar, raffle, silent auction or other activities.

Halloween

Halloween, a contraction of All Hallow's Evening, is held on 31 October – the eve of the feast of All Hallows, or All Saints' Day. It's traditionally a time of remembering dead saints and martyrs but is now synonymous with dressing up as ghouls, witches and skeletons, trick or treating and pumpkin Jack-o'-lanterns.

- **Sell Halloween treats to friends and colleagues.** Bake cupcakes and transform them into spiders' webs, skeletons, mummies, broomsticks, Jack-o'-lanterns or other Halloween horrors. Add a few meringue 'ghosts'.
- **Hold a Halloween party.** Decorate your venue with crêpe paper pumpkin images, black and orange streamers and some of the glowing or flashing Halloween novelties on sale in supermarkets and joke shops. Encourage your guests to come in fancy dress and award prizes for the best male and female costumes. Serve spicy tomato soup, sausages and jacket potatoes, baked apples and Halloween cakes and bakes. Charge for tickets and sell glow sticks and bracelets, sweets and soft drinks. Play plenty of games.
  - o **Apple bobbing.** Players have to retrieve an apple out of a tub of water without using their hands.
  - o **Tower of flour.** Fill a pudding bowl with flour and turn it upside down onto a plate to make a 'tower'. Place a chocolate or other sweet at the top of the tower. Each person takes it in turn to cut or scoop out a slice from the tower. The player who makes the tower collapse has to pick up the sweet from the plate with their mouth. Have plenty of aprons, face wipes and towels to hand!
  - o **Mummy wrap.** Party goers pair up and each team is given a roll of toilet paper. One person spins the other around, covering them in paper until they are turned into a mummy. The first team to finish wins.
  - o **Pumpkin skittles.** Set up skittles made from screw-top plastic bottles filled with water. Use small to medium-sized pumpkins as balls. The team which knocks down the most skittles wins.
  - o **Sweet moves.** Give each player a small bowl of sweets, an empty bowl and a spoon. Participants have to move the sweets from one bowl to the other using only the spoon in their mouth.

147

Bonfire night

Remember, remember the fifth of November, Gunpowder treason and plot! Bonfire night celebrates the discovery and thwarting of the 'Gunpowder Plot' by Guy Fawkes and others to blow up the Houses of Parliament in 1605. Images of Guy Fawkes, or 'guys' have been burned on bonfires on 5 November ever since.

Many charities, councils, schools and sports clubs already run annual bonfire night fundraisers. If there is already a well-established event in your town or village, approach the organisers to see if you can collaborate by providing refreshments or running complementary activities.

If there's no established event in your area, you may want to consider holding your own. The Health and Safety Executive (www.hse. gov.uk) has published two guides, which you can download free of charge from their website or buy at www.hsebooks.co.uk or any good bookshop.

The first, *Giving your own firework display* has been written for organisers who want to run the event and light the fireworks themselves but have no specialist knowledge. It gives guidance on firework regulations, selecting a site, facilities needed at the site, storing fireworks safely, crowd control, bonfire safety, firing the display and clearing up afterwards. It also gives advice on liaising with the fire service, police, coastguard, Civil Aviation Authority and other bodies.

The second publication, *Working together on firework displays: A guide to safety for firework display organisers and operators* is for competent display operators and organisers who are able to set up and fire larger and more powerful fireworks than those available to the general public.

If you want to buy, keep and use fireworks in Northern Ireland (except for indoor fireworks and sparklers) you must obtain a fireworks licence issued by the Department of Justice for Northern Ireland (www.dojni.gov.uk).

Start organising the display as early as possible and give particular roles to specific volunteers. Roles will need to include: insurance and risk assessment; ordering, storing and setting off the fireworks; liaising with neighbours, the fire service and other bodies; publicising the event; crowd control; and site facilities. Will there be a bonfire? If so, talk to your local authority environmental protection department. Does your venue have catering facilities so you can serve tasty soup, jacket potatoes, hot dogs, toffee apples and hot drinks? Charge for tickets – it's common practice to offer a discount on tickets bought ahead of the event – and sell them at the door. Sell glow sticks and think about what other fundraising activities you can include – bearing in mind it will be dark.

Get supporters to dig out their old clothes and make guys. Ask local traders and residents to help promote the event by putting them in their shop windows or front gardens.

St Andrew's Day

St Andrew, the patron saint of Scotland, was a Galilean fisherman, who with his brother Simon Peter became a disciple of Jesus Christ. He is believed to have been executed by the Romans on an X-shaped cross. The X-shaped cross (Saltire) is the national emblem and flag of the Scots and St Andrew's Day (30 November) is marked with a celebration of Scottish culture and food.

Raise money by celebrating all things Scottish.

- **St Andrew's Day dinner.** It doesn't have to be haggis, neeps and tatties – save them for Burns' night. How about a starter of Scottish smoked salmon, Cullen Skink, Scotch broth, or cock-a-leekie soup? Serve roast Aberdeen Angus beef, venison, grouse or lamb, with something for your vegetarians to enjoy as well. Follow up with a pudding of Scottish raspberries and cream, raspberry cranachan, whisky trifle, marmalade and whisky sponge or bannocks (oatcakes) and cheese. Ask volunteers to help prepare the food, hire an outside caterer or team up with a local pub, hotel or restaurant for an agreed split of the profits. Decorate the room with all things Scottish – photos of landmarks, men in kilts, bagpipes, thistles, and the Saltire. If you know anyone who can play the bagpipes, book them as early as possible.
- **Scottish afternoon tea or coffee morning.** Invite friends and neighbours into your home to enjoy homemade shortbread, Selkirk Bannock loaf (Scottish fruit loaf), Scotch pancakes and Dundee cake. Take your cakes and bakes into work and sell them to your colleagues to enjoy with their morning coffee or afternoon tea.
- **Whisky tasting.** Team up with a local pub or hotel and invite guests to enjoy an evening spent sampling Scottish whiskies.
- **Scottish country dancing.** See if there's a local group you can book to give a display of Scottish dancing or run your own 'ceil-dlh' (see Barn dance) and serve themed refreshments to your guests.
- **Sponsored kilt wearing.** Lads – ask colleagues to sponsor you to wear a kilt to work. But beware! The lassies are bound to ask what, if anything, you're wearing under your kilt! Tell them they can find out if they can raise a certain amount in sponsorship by a set time – and remember to wear the brightest pair of swimming trunks or shorts you own!

Christmas

Christmas is a great time to fundraise. Carol singing, gift wrapping and decorated Christmas trees are all part of the fun and build-up to the big day (25 December). People will be seeking out gifts and stocking fillers as well as greenery and other decorations for their homes and dinner tables.

Craft fairs do particularly well at Christmas, so you might want to consider running your own or hiring a stall at another charity or organisation's event.

- **Hold a Christmas tree festival.**
- **Deck the halls.** Do you have a friendly landowner, farmer or gardener who will let you cut any mistletoe, holly or other seasonal greenery on their land? Gather and sell the greenery quite close to Christmas to keep it fresh. Sell the mistletoe in small bunches and the holly in bags (make sure there are plenty of berries!). Make table decorations from the smaller pieces, adding fir cones, candles, small baubles and ribbon.
- **Christmas wreaths.** Welcome wreaths date back to Roman times, when they were thought to bring good luck to the household. They are usually made from evergreens such as fir, oak and eucalyptus to symbolise strength, as evergreens retain their leaves through even the harshest of winters. Form your basic shape from polystyrene, oasis, circles of wire – recycle your old wire coat hangers – or thin sticks, vines or willow. Stick or twist the greenery into the frame and decorate with pine cones, small dried oranges or clementines, baubles, and bows. Do a selection of wreaths – for some the more decorations you can pile on the better, for others, less is more! How about making candy wreaths

from brightly wrapped sweets and chocolates? Sell at fairs or to friends and work colleagues. A wreath would also make a great raffle prize at a Christmas event or a lot to sell at auction.

- **Christmas trees.** Church, village hall and sports club car parks are ideal places for drivers to pull in and buy trees. You could buy the trees from a local plantation and recruit volunteers to sell them or invite a tree seller to use your venue in return for a percentage of the takings. Advertise, advertise, advertise!
- **Christmas fairs and other events.** Add some additional festive fundraisers.
  - **Pluck a turkey.** Like 'lucky straws' (see Fairs and fun days). Stick your straws into a paper mache or polystyrene 'turkey'.
  - **Lucky stockings.** Collect brightly coloured (washed) socks and put small gifts in each one. Peg them on a line and charge people to pick a sock.
  - **Pin a red nose on Rudolf the reindeer** – instead of a tail on a donkey.
  - **Snow ball fun.** Paint a snowman on a large sheet of MDF, hardboard or thick cardboard and make a hole where his nose should be. Make snowballs out of scrunched paper or use table tennis balls. Award small prizes depending on how many snowballs participants manage to throw through the hole.
  - **Santa's grotto.** Young children love the idea of visiting Santa in his grotto and receiving an early Christmas gift. Your grotto doesn't have to be too elaborate – why not cover a garden gazebo in old sheets which have been painted to look like a log cabin wall and decorate it with fairy lights? Find a nice big chair for Santa and a bench or small seats for his visitors to sit on. Give him a couple of sacks filled with presents wrapped in different colours for boys and girls and different age groups. Recruit some elves or fairies – one to take the money, another to manage any queue and a third to stay with Santa for safeguarding purposes. Wherever possible use helpers or

members of staff who have already undergone a Disclosure and Barring Service check (Disclosure Scotland in Scotland, AccessNi in Northern Ireland) through their employment or a voluntary role to act as Santa and his assistants. A parent should remain with their child at all times. It's best practice for Santa to be accompanied by at least one other adult at all times and to ensure that he is never placed in unaccompanied one-to-one contact with a child in a private place such as a grotto. Bear in mind that each visit may take around three to four minutes, so if your event's lasting two hours, Santa could see about 40 children.

- **Gift wrapping.** It's surprising how many people love buying gifts but hate wrapping them. Ask a shopping mall, arcade or department store if you can set up a gift wrapping service and charge per item. Have a selection of different papers and gift tags. Set charges according to the size of the gifts and charge extra for bows and rosettes. Make sure you've plenty of scissors, gift wrap, bubble wrap, rolls of sticky tape and ribbon. Find an 'expert' to give your wrappers some advance training.
- **Mince pies, Christmas cakes, puddings and other festive fare.** Bake and sell at your events, car boot sales (if terms and conditions allow), and take to work to sell to colleagues.
- **Carol singing.** Approach your local bus station, railway station, shopping mall and pubs. Ask if they would let you sing carols for your cause. Go carol singing door-to-door or pub-to-pub (see Street and door-to-door collections).
- **Hold a carolathon.** (See Hymnathon and sing carols.)
- **Santas galore!** Take advantage of the festive season by encouraging your volunteers to dress as Santas, snowmen, elves and fairies, etc at your stalls and events. They'll draw attention and extra sales. Hold a sponsored Santa or snowman run, walk, or cycle ride. Make sure the event begins and ends at your venue and sell, sell, sell!

Celebrate your own special date

Getting married? Celebrating a significant birthday, wedding anniversary or retirement? If relatives, friends or colleagues want to give you a present, suggest they make a donation to your cause or charity instead.

***

See also: How do I make it safe and legal?; Alcohol (liquor) licensing; Food safety; Licensing – playing live and recorded music; Sponsorship; Auctions and Lotteries and non-commercial gaming and betting.

12
Brain teasers

Fun quiz

Holding a fun quiz is a relatively simple way to raise funds. They're easy to organise, can be scaled up or down depending on the number of participants, and can be tailored to suit particular guests – older people, families, sports enthusiasts, etc – or celebrations such as Christmas or St George's Day.

A successful quiz depends on getting the right quizmaster and setting the right questions. A good quizmaster will have presence, head teacher-like control and, if necessary, be able to lay down the law. Match your questions to your target audience. They should be sufficiently challenging, easy to understand and interesting enough that people will want to know the correct answer.

An average quiz night lasts for two to three hours and usually comprises eight rounds of 8–10 questions with a break in the middle, when you can serve refreshments. Make sure you've got enough questions to keep the quiz going and involve the quizmaster in setting the questions – they'll need to understand the questions they're posing. Research your own questions or use questions from quiz books or websites.

Pick from themes such as film and TV, famous people, science, history, geography, general knowledge and myths and legends. Add a couple of extra games that teams can work on between rounds and are marked at the end. This could be a photo round with pictures of famous people, company logos or unusual objects which teams have to identify, or anagrams of capital cities, rivers or other names.

Church and school halls, social clubs and pubs all make good venues. Most quizzes involve teams of between two and eight people. Each team will need a marking sheet with the name of the round and numbered spaces for each answer. Set some rules, for example banning the use of mobile 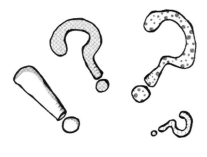 phones and the internet. Mark after each round. This establishes who is in the lead and instigates some friendly rivalry.

The winners won't expect more than a token prize if they know it's a charity event. Award a cash prize that team members can share or individual prizes such as bottles of wine (over 18s only), sweets or shopping vouchers.

Raise money by charging an entry fee per person or team (perhaps with a discount for families), seeking sponsors for each round of questions, selling refreshments (or including them in your entry fee), and adding a raffle or other activities.

Spelling bee

Take your guests back to their school days by holding a spelling bee. Divide your participants into teams of between two and four people and provide each team with a whiteboard, blackboard or sheets of A4 paper.

Work out the words you want people to spell in advance, starting with easier words in the early rounds and getting progressively more difficult. Involve the compère in the selection, so they're able to pronounce each word and put it in context. Words or rounds could be themed – for example names from the Bible, adjectives or words ending in 'ent' or 'ant'.

As each word is given, give teams 30 seconds to spell the answer. When a bell or buzzer sounds, or on the command of the compère, the teams have to reveal their spellings.

You could run your bee as a quiz and award a prize to the team with the most correct spellings at the end of the evening, or gradually eliminate teams until you have a winner.

If you like the idea of a spelling bee, but aren't sure how many other people would share your idea of fun, why not test it out by incorporating a spelling round into a general quiz?

Who's that baby?

Guessing whether that baby is now your boss, head teacher or vicar is great fun as a money raiser on its own or run as part of a larger event. Ask prominent members of your school, church, business or other organisation to bring in a photograph of themselves as a baby or young child as well as a current picture. You'll need between 12 and 20 photographs to make the competition worthwhile. If possible, expand the pictures to A5 size and mount them on a display board or wall. Give each baby picture a number and each current photo a letter.

Ask people to buy an entry form on which they try to match the baby photos to the grown-ups. Reveal the true identities of the babies at the end of the event. If there is more than one correct entry, hold a draw to select the winner.

Murder mystery night

Invite your guests to turn detective by holding your very own murder mystery event.

Search online for a team to run the drama for you, or, if your supporters include budding thespians, buy a game online and enact it yourselves. There are game packs available for 6–200 guests. The packs should include invitations, the background to the drama, a step-by-step guide to staging the performance, scripts and clues as well as profiles of the individual characters.

If you want to stage your event at home, you can buy boxed games for up to 12 players from high street retailers and online.

Start the evening with a pre-dinner drinks 'meet and greet' reception where the characters introduce themselves. The performance is then played out between dinner courses with each table deciding whodunit. Ask guests to dress up in line with the theme of the drama you have chosen and award prizes for the best costumes. Sell tickets and, depending on the size of your event, add a raffle or silent auction.

Beetle drive

Beetle drives are really easy to organise and provide an enjoyable way to meet new people. All you need is a room with tables and chairs, beetle sheets with 9–12 boxes for people to draw their beetles in, dice, shakers, pencils and a set of instructions on how to play for each table.

Group players in tables of four. Each person takes a turn to throw the die. Once they have thrown a six they can draw the body of their beetle and then add limbs, eyes, antennae, etc according to which number they throw. As soon as a player completes their beetle they shout 'beetle'. All players then stop and add up the number of body parts they have managed to add to their own beetle, scoring one point for each part. The player with the highest score on each table then moves to the next table in a clockwise direction while the player with the lowest score moves anti-clockwise. As soon as everyone is sitting at their new table, another round begins. This continues for however many rounds you decide or time allows.

Ask players to keep a running total of their scores. Award a prize to the player who has the highest score at the end of the final game. If a number of players have the same score, roll a die to determine the overall winner. Winners of individual rounds could also be given small prizes – perhaps a chocolate beetle or ladybird.

Hold a break halfway through and sell hot and cold drinks, sweets and snacks or include a hot supper in the entrance fee.

***

See also: How do I make it safe and legal?; Alcohol (liquor) licensing; Food safety; Auctions and Lotteries and non-commercial gaming and betting.

Useful contacts and resources

Find your local council (England only) www.gov.uk/find-your-local-council	
Disclosure and Barring Service (England and Wales) www.gov.uk/dbs 0870 909 0811 Email: customerservices@dbs.gsi.gov.uk	Disclosure and Barring Service Customer Services PO Box 110 Liverpool L69 3JD
Disclosure Scotland (Scotland) www.disclosurescotland.co.uk 0870 609 6006 Email: info@disclosurescotland.co.uk	Disclosure Scotland PO Box 250 Glasgow G51 1YU
AccessNi (Northern Ireland) www.nidirect.gov.uk/accessni 0300 200 7888 Email: accessni@ani.x.gsi.gov.uk	AccessNi PO Box 1085 Belfast BT5 9BD
Health and Safety Executive www.hse.gov.uk 0300 003 1747 Email: advice@hse.gsi.gov.uk Provides guides to health, safety and welfare at events which can be purchased or downloaded free of charge.	Health and Safety Executive Redgrave Court Merton Road Bootle Liverpool L20 7HS
Health and Safety Executive Northern Ireland www.hseni.gov.uk 0289 024 3249 Email: mail@hseni.gov.uk	Health and Safety Executive Northern Ireland Belfast HQ 83 Ladas Drive Belfast BT6 9FR

National Society for the Prevention of Cruelty to Children www.nspcc.org.uk Information and helpline: 0808 800 5000 Email: help@nspcc.org.uk Children's charity fighting to end child abuse in the UK and Channel Islands. Provides advice on preventing abuse and keeping children safe.	National Society for the Prevention of Cruelty to Children Weston House 42 Curtain Road London EC2A 3NH
St John Ambulance www.sja.org.uk 0870 010 4950	St John Ambulance 27 St John's Lane London EC1M 4BU
British Red Cross www.redcross.org.uk 0844 871 1111 Email: information@redcross.org.uk	British Red Cross UK Office 44 Moorfields London EC2Y 9AL
Food Standards Agency www.food.gov.uk 0207 276 8829 Email: helpline@foodstandards.gsi.gov.uk Catering advice for charities and community groups providing food.	Food Standards Agency UK HQ Aviation House 125 Kingsway London WC2B 6NH
HM Revenue & Customs www.hmrc.gov.uk Charities Helpline: 0300 123 1073 Email: charities@hmrc.gov.uk **Gift Aid** www.hmrc.gov.uk/charities/gift_aid Information on Gift Aid and VAT on sponsorship payments to charities.	HM Revenue & Customs Charity Correspondence, S0708 PO Box 205 Bootle Liverpool L69 9AZ

Filmbank Distributors Ltd www.filmbank.co.uk 0207 984 5957 Email: info@filmbank.co.uk Licenses the screening of films outside the home or cinema.	Filmbank Distributors Ltd Warner House 98 Theobald's Road WC1X 8WB
PRS for Music www.prsformusic.com 0207 580 5544 Collects and pays royalties on behalf of song writers, composers and publishers, whenever a song or composition they have written is played or performed in public.	PRS for Music 2 Pancras Square Kings Cross London N1C 4AG
Phonographic Performance Ltd (PPL) www.ppluk.com 0207 534 1000 Email: info@ppluk.com Licenses recorded music played in public or broadcast.	Phonographic Performance Ltd 1 Upper James Street London W1F 9DE
Gambling Commission www.gamblingcommission.gov.uk 0121 230 6666 Email: info@gamblingcommission.co.uk	Gambling Commission Victoria Square House Victoria Square Birmingham B2 4BP
Social Policy Unit, Department for Social Development www.dsdni.gov.uk 0289 082 9521 Email: social.policy@dsdni.gov.uk Information about gambling, liquor licensing and street trading in Northern Ireland.	Social Policy Unit, Department for Social Development 4th Floor, Lighthouse Building 1 Cromac Place Gasworks Business Park Ormeau Road Belfast BT7 2JB

Royal Automobile Club Competition Authorisation Office www.msauk.org 0175 376 5000 Authorising body for all motor events held on the public highway in England and Wales.	The Royal Automobile Club Competition Authorisation Office Motor Sports House Riverside Park Colnbrook Slough SL3 0HG
RSAC Motorsport Limited www.rsacmotorsport.co.uk 0843 289 3953 Authorising body for all motor events held on the public highway in Scotland.	RSAC Motorsport Limited PO Box 3333 Glasgow G20 2AX
Northern Ireland Council for Voluntary Action www.nicva.org 0289 087 7777 Email: cas@nicva.org Membership and representative body for the voluntary and community sector in Northern Ireland. Provides information and guidance to fundraisers.	NICVA 61 Duncairn Gardens Belfast BT15 2GB
Institute of Fundraising www.institute-of-fundraising.org.uk 0207 840 1000 Email: info@institute-of-fundraising.org.uk Professional body for UK fundraisers. Provides legal and best practice guidance.	Institute of Fundraising Charter House 13–15 Carteret Street London SW1H 9DJ
PTA-UK www.pta.org.uk 0300 123 5460 Email: info@pta.org.uk Charitable organisation supporting Parent Teacher Associations in England, Wales and Northern Ireland. Ideas, information and guidance for parents and staff.	PTA-UK 39 Shipbourne Road Tonbridge Kent TN10 3DS

About the author

Penny Hallett has more than 40 years' experience in journalism, public relations, and marketing. She spent the majority of her career in the public sector, where she imagined and brought to life many national, regional, and local awareness-raising campaigns and events, several of which won prestigious industry awards.

She started fundraising when she was 10, writing a magazine and selling it to friends and classmates to raise money for disadvantaged children. The free sweet with each copy boosted sales enormously!

Penny is currently working as a volunteer with the St Michael's Church Heart of the Community project. The project aims to raise £5.5 million to build a new church and community centre, restore the 14th century church, and refurbish the Old School Rooms at Stoke Gifford, South Gloucestershire, UK. All royalties from the sale of this book are being donated to the project.

15935947R00099

Printed in Great Britain
by Amazon